CHRISTOPHER MARTIN
'In the Middle of the Music'

Like Christopher Martin, Mary Ryllis Clark migrated to Australia twice, first in 1974 and secondly in 1980. Returning to England in between, she wrote her first book, *Crown of a Thousand Years* (1978). Those written in Australia include *Altered Lives — Personal Experiences of Schizophrenia* (1994), *Discover Historic Victoria* (1996), *Timbertop — Celebrating 50 Years* (2003) and *Loreto in Australia* (2009).

CHRISTOPHER MARTIN
'In the Middle of the Music'

Memoir & Memories

edited by
Mary Ryllis Clark

ARCADIA

© Mary Ryllis Clark 2012

First published 2012, by Arcadia
the general books' imprint of Australian Scholarly Publishing Pty Ltd
7 Lt Lothian St Nth, North Melbourne, Vic 3051   TEL: 03 9329 6963   FAX: 03 9329 5452
EMAIL: aspic@ozemail.com.au   WEB: scholarly.info

ISBN 978-1-921875-84-7

Cover design Art Rowlands   *Typesetting* Sarah Anderson
Printing and binding BPA Print Group

The main chapters of this book are typeset in Minion Pro 11pt

Contents

Preface & Acknowledgements

For a born storyteller, Christopher Martin was surprisingly reluctant to embark on a memoir. It was Jasmine Brunner's enthusiasm and commitment that gave birth to the project: in December 2010, some months after he had celebrated his eightieth birthday, she suggested to Chris that he could talk and I would write. Tired and already feeling the effects of the leukaemia that ten months later would take his life, Chris hesitated.

Chris' great friend, Miki Pohl, encouraged him to meet me and talk about it. Miki was to prove central to the writing of this memoir. The three of us gathered at Chris's flat in Toorak on a Saturday morning shortly before Christmas. Chris was sitting in his armchair, nervous, even a little suspicious. When he learned that I, too, was British and shared his love of Gilbert and Sullivan and Elgar, the pomp and pageantry of monarchy and stony beaches, we were off. He launched into his story about Imogen Holst and the Amadeus String Quartet and spoke for an hour, hardly pausing for breath.

This was the pattern of our meetings. They would take place on a Saturday or Sunday morning so that Miki Pohl could be present filming, or sometimes Chris and I would get together on a weekday with Annette, who brought ginger biscuits. Chris would always be sitting in his armchair, often weary to begin with (initially he was having blood transfusions every three weeks) until he picked up a thread, usually provided by Miki. The colour would come back to his face as he warmed to his theme and soon he was in full flight, occasionally getting up to find a book to look something up or to point to a photograph to illustrate a story.

I visited Chris regularly for six months. There were times when he would call and say he just wasn't up to it. When he was up to it, he was like a spring pouring from a mountainside, with rivulets of distraction breaking away from the main stream tumbling off at tangents.

Inevitably there are big gaps in the narrative. To some extent, these have been filled in by his family and those friends who have contributed to the 'Memories' section of this book. I am deeply grateful to them for sharing their recollections so generously and creating a context for Chris's own words. Every one of them spoke with great affection for Chris and each provides a different insight into this complex and inspiring man. His musicianship and empathetic personality clearly touched the lives of thousands of people beyond his immediate family and friends – people he has played music with over his lifetime, his colleagues and students, the orchestra, players he conducted and his audiences.

Chris Martin's memoir has been supported from the beginning by a great deal of generosity. It would not have happened without the commission from Jasmine Brunner and support of Miki Pohl. Annette Martin has been gracious and helpful with information and the loan of family photographs. Unless otherwise stated, all the images in the book are from the Martin family collection. Benjamin Martin provided feedback on the text, headings for the different 'Memories' and words for the Interval and Coda sections.

Thanks to my friend Jill Fenwick for her editorial support and encouragement. Maria Vandamme and Ian Perry were endlessly patient with questions about music and musicians. Miranda Fyfield kindly supplied information about Music in the Round. Thanks too to Jasmine Brunner, Annette Martin, Miki Pohl, Hartmut Lindemann, Henry Wenig, Dona Dening and Heather O'Connor for reading and commenting on the text. Thanks to Miki Pohl, Rowan Thomas, Phillip Antippa and Corpus Medicorum for their financial contribution to the book's production and to Helen Sykes for sponsoring an eBook. Allan Kleiman transformed the damaged cover image and Hannah Raines did a fine job transcribing many hours of recordings.

I am most grateful to Nick Walker and his team: Dr Diane Carlyle for her careful editing, Sarah Anderson for her elegant design, and Terryn Whiteoak and Art Rowlands for pulling everything together.

Mary Ryllis Clark

Introduction

Christopher Martin was a serious, vulnerable and gentle man. He had a gravitas in his nature that informed everything. He was a deep thinker, a searcher for knowledge, understanding and beauty. Music was his passion, his life's work, and his love of music, his engine.

Chris's life in music was distinguished by its variety and breadth. He played viola as his first instrument, and knew the string quartet and orchestral repertoire intimately. His violin playing and teaching were exemplary in their imaginative creativity. He loved his teaching, and his colleagues. He gave of himself in his teaching, with his gift for seeing through straight to the essence of the music. And as a conductor, he conveyed his pleasure in the score, with tremendous wit, humour, passion and humanity.

He was inspired by greatness in playing, honesty and passion in artists, past and present. He could be scathing about 'stupid' playing, and alongside his gentleness he could be really strict, and tough when faced with situations that dismayed him.

Everybody loved Chris. How was it possible to do otherwise? He was gently kind, thoughtful and funny. His humour was famous – a great gift to us all, in rehearsals, at dinner, travelling, wherever. Chris would have a joke or a story to share, to defuse any tension, to entertain, or when just simply being Chris.

He was able to see the funny side of life, the little quirks in people. He was great company. Tremendously human, his kindnesses touched us all. He brewed a wonderful pot of tea, loved a wee tot of fine whisky.

He loved his family beyond words.

We miss him terribly.

Elizabeth Wallfisch (née Hunt)

PART 1

Memoir

Imogen Holst once told me something amazing. She asked if I knew the four songs that her father had written for voice and violin. I knew them well and had played them often. 'I think they are my father's greatest work', she said. 'There is nothing more personal in his music than those four little songs.' I was shocked as the whole set only lasts about ten minutes. Imogen was the daughter of the great Gustav Holst, a man who wrote marvellous music including *The Planets* and *Egdon Heath* and his daughter thought these four simple songs his finest work![1]

Imo, as we always called her, explained the story behind the songs. Her father had a close association with the lovely village of Thaxted, in Essex, where the family lived for a while.[2] It had a remarkably fine parish church where Holst played the organ. On one occasion, he wandered in and found a woman walking up the aisles playing the violin and singing. She wasn't using words, just soaring sounds that resonated with the notes of the violin. This is a technique known as 'sonority'. It's about the voice getting inside the violin. It's an extraordinary thing. The violin plays a note and you sing a sixth and you can get a chord, a humming, in the upper frequencies.

The woman was completely absorbed in her music and Holst was so taken with the sound that he decided to write songs for voice and violin using the same technique. Both parts – the voice and violin   are quite simple; it's the sonority that makes them special. You can't explain what happens. The voice and the notes merge. Of course in a church – a big church like Thaxted – it's more noticeable. The voice has to be choir-boy pure, the singer intelligent enough to sing with the equally pure notes of the violin. Interestingly, they are not pieces for big soloists. Joan Sutherland's magnificent voice and Yehudi Menuhin's warm rich tone, for example, wouldn't be right.

These works are not fashionable, you can't build your reputation on them, but I play them a lot because I love them. A lush vibrato can be wonderful but it's not what Holst wanted. It's only when you get the purity of sound that it works. I once played these pieces with a singer who was perfect. When she sang, the fiddle trembled; it shook with sonority. The most famous story of this sort of thing is about Caruso's breaking glass with the vibration of his voice. Imo was her father's daughter and knew his music inside out. I find it fascinating that she picked those four songs. To me, they represent total immersion in music.

Browsing through my books the other day I came across one on the Amadeus Quartet, my idols when I was younger. Now so famous, their first concert at the Wigmore Hall was financed by Imogen, not knowing if it was going to be a success. In fact, there were long queues down Wigmore Street. The quartet had been playing together for a few months and their friends knew how good they were, but it was Imo who launched them. She was a fine musician and eccentric, rather like Edith Sitwell. She always wore an Indian sari, with her hair pulled back.

When I went to Dartington for the first time, I met the Amadeus Quartet.³ They welcomed me so enthusiastically that I was confused. It turned out the name 'Christopher Martin' was important to them. He was the first administrator there and very special to the place. He died in 1944 and the Amadeus was preparing a concert in his honour. The people at Dartington always took an interest in me because of the name. It was like a reincarnation!

On that first visit, I also met Imo. We had a mutual friend at the Royal College, an elderly violinist called Sybil Eaton. Imo was then living at Aldeburgh and did a lot of the donkey work for Benjamin Britten. She also put on the occasional Sunday afternoon concert and asked me if I had a group which could come and play. My then girlfriend played the flute and we had a friend who sometimes played the cello with us.

The three of us would go down to Aldeburgh and rehearse in Ben Britten's house with Peter Pears. Peter would sing early music, Bach or Schütz and so on, with two or three strings and perhaps an organ. Imo put together the programme for these Sunday concerts and the locals loved them. Ben was always there but rarely played, except to accompany Peter occasionally. One day as we were rehearsing, Ben walked in, asked what we were playing and if we wanted to play a quartet. He was a marvellous pianist. I remember saying to myself, 'Christ, Ben Britten is sitting here playing with us!'

From local shopkeepers to international big-wigs, everyone always knew him as 'Ben'. The first time we met, I was a lowly student and called him 'Mr Britten' but he said, 'Call me Ben'. That's what he wanted; nobody called him 'Mr Britten'. Peter Pears would tease him about this. He was always 'Peter', never 'Pete'.

To begin at the beginning

My father, Frank, was a bricklayer from Dulverton, a very lovely small town in Somerset, right on Exmore. His family had always been from that part of the country – Devon and Somerset – and he was born there in 1890. My mother, Sarah, came from the village of Woodford not far from Manchester. Her northern accent was particularly noticeable on the phone, though I was unaware of it when I was with her. She'd say, 'Yr' right, luv? Yr lookin' aff-ter y'rself, luv?' I adored my mother; she was wonderful. She loved music and played 'Jesus Loves Me, This I Know Because the Bible Tells Me So' and other Salvation Army hymns on the piano at home, and sang her heart out. We all loved it, even Dad, who didn't know anything about music whatsoever.

My parents met in Liverpool during World War I, when my father was convalescing from war wounds. His surname was Martin and my mother's was Partridge – both English birds. My father had a shocking time in the war and was wounded three times. When he shaved, you could see the shrapnel embedded in his arm. It was deep but I don't think that he was in pain. When he was taken back to base, the surgeon told him that his arm had to come off or he would die. There were hundreds of wounded men to deal with and he didn't have the time to try to save it. But Dad refused to have his arm amputated and one of the nurses offered to look after him. She dressed and cleaned the wound for hours every night and it came good. It healed. There was a bit of shrapnel in one of Dad's legs and in one eye. This gave him trouble later on and he eventually lost his sight in that eye. He should have got compensation but he didn't.

My mother was just twenty-one when they married in 1921, ten years younger than Dad. She had a hard time because they had to live with his parents. He was the youngest of two boys and his mother's favourite. Nobody was going to be good enough for him, nobody. She wasn't very kind to my mother and spoilt my father no end. He did what he liked. One of the worst things for my mother was the fifty canaries that he kept in the bedroom. He was usually out at night, hanging around with his football or cricket friends – though he never drank with them – and my mother would be in the bedroom by herself, with the mice and rats scratching around because the birds chucked seed everywhere. She hated it.

My sister, Betty, was born there in 1925. She died recently, at the age of eighty-four. She had dementia in the end, but seemed quite happy and imagined that she was talking to our parents all the time. I saw her the year before she died and she didn't know who I was. It was sad in one way but not in another. Previously it had always been painful to say goodbye, as we never knew when we would see each other again. This time she called out, 'Cheerio!', without giving it a thought.

When Betty was four, we moved to a tiny little house in Tiverton, in Devon, where Dad found work as a bricklayer. The town had a population of about 10,000, about half of whom worked in the local lace factory. It was famous for its lace and, after the war, made the lace for Princess Elizabeth's wedding veil. Our house, which is still there, had a shop in front and my parents rented the rest of the building, one room downstairs and two small bedrooms upstairs. There was gas but no electricity. The lavatory was outside and was freezing at any time, but in winter it was unbelievable. Every Saturday night, my father brought in the big metal bath from outside. I had a wash first before bed and then my sister did, and I suppose that my parents would have a bath too, after us. I don't know. I stayed under the bedcovers. For the rest of the week, we'd just have a wash.

That's how it was until we moved into a council house when I was four. Council houses weren't wonderful but they were alright. We had three little bedrooms and a bathroom. We kept to the same routine of having a bath once a week, on a Saturday, though in a proper bath. My mother lived in that house for the rest of her life and died there 1986.

War broke out in 1939 and the blackout was eerie and frightening. At the slightest chink of light, the wardens came knocking on the door yelling, 'Put that light out! Put that light out!' Evidently from the air, you can see the tiniest chink of light. We didn't have an air-raid shelter and we didn't really expect Tiverton to be bombed, but it did get a few hits. One bomb landed on the workhouse and killed a couple of people. Whenever the siren went, my mother got me and my sister up and took us down to the triangular little room under the stairs. She gave us tea and biscuits and we'd sit there until the all-clear went. Dad wouldn't get up, even though Mum used to call out, 'Come on, Frankie'. He said that he'd got through World War I and wasn't going to bother with this one. 'If I'm going to die, I'll do it in bed', he said.

I was usually half-asleep but it was exciting. Exeter, about fourteen miles from us, had two consecutive nights of horrific bombing and we heard it all. One wing of the cathedral was extensively damaged and later rebuilt. Both Tiverton and Exeter had military bases, and towards the end of the war a terrific contingent of Americans came to town. They camped on the recreation ground near us and didn't behave terribly well, seducing all the girls, some of whom ran off with them. The Germans must have known that they were there, but they were never bombed. Plymouth and Portsmouth, the two big naval bases, got a huge pounding.

In the meantime, I was at school and doing quite well until I met Ron Davey. He changed my life. Ron had worked at Morris Motors in Oxford for nine years and loved it. He was an amateur violinist and played with the Oxford Light Orchestra. It was quite a respectable orchestra. Sir Thomas Beecham came and conducted its concerts occasionally. Ron indulged his love of music by going to concerts in the Ashmolean Museum and other theatres and concert halls and heard everybody he could.

Ron had an autograph book as big as a church bible, about six inches thick, choc-a-block with hundreds of autographs from all kinds of famous people, including Gandhi. He was the greatest storyteller I have ever known. He once showed me the autograph of Evangeline Booth, daughter of the founder of the Salvation Army, and told me that he'd gone to hear her talk. Afterwards he joined a queue of people waiting to meet her and found himself ushered into a little room where she asked him to pray with her. He did and then she signed his book. Things like that happened to Ron, as he wasn't afraid to go and talk to famous people and they didn't generally mind. His black autograph book would be a treasure trove of incredible stories. I think he left it to his son.

In Oxford, Ron got to know Lord Nuffield, founder of Morris Motors, who had started life in a bicycle shop and became one of the greatest, richest car manufacturers ever. He was a very approachable man, a man of the people, and Ron knew him well and he helped Ron to get some of his autographs. Ron also had a few Christmas and greetings cards from royalty and said that the Duke of Marlborough had given them to him to add to his autograph collection. That book took on a life of its own.

Ron went back to his native Tiverton when war broke out, because his health wasn't good enough for him to join the forces. He got work in a garage and started playing his violin for local events. I used to pass his place on the way to school and we always said hello. Everybody did in those days, in a small town like Tiverton. One of the teachers at my primary school had taught a group of us violin for a year when I was ten. She used to say, 'Anyone who wants to learn, can learn', but we lost interest. Mum was keen for me to go back to it – always hopeful that it could lead to something good. She heard Ron playing in a concert and went up to him afterwards and asked if he would teach me. Ron agreed, even though he had never taught anyone before. It was the start of a lifelong friendship. Ron always had faith in me, always.

Ron gave me such a passion for the violin and for music, that schoolwork was completely pushed aside. I didn't care about it and rushed through my homework before leaving school so that it wouldn't interfere with my violin time. I had a lesson nearly every night. I wasn't dumb, I just couldn't get into my studies and didn't want to. The teachers used to get pretty angry. In Lower 4B, I was at the bottom of my class. My report read, 'Reaches usual low standard, 33/33'. Dad was furious. 'Right, that's it', he said. 'You're hopeless, useless, you'll be pushing barrels up a plank.' He had no faith in me at all, took me out of school and put me in the lace factory. I was just sixteen. My sister had been working there since she was fourteen. She started in 1939, the year war broke out and the factory switched from making lace to making parachutes. It was important work and lives depended on it. Betty said that they were terribly careful to fold parachutes the right way, because otherwise they wouldn't open.

The war was ending in 1945 when I started in the engineering section of the factory, making tiny brass wheels that held the lace in place. The lace-making areas were full of the noise and clatter of machines. You couldn't hear yourself speak and everyone lip-read. There were thousands of people working there and the owners were good to their workers, paid them well and treated them with respect. They had a co-partnership system whereby the workers shared in the profits and everybody got a bonus at Christmas.

The factory was owned by Sir John Heathcoat Amory and his brother
Derick, and it had been in the family since 1816. Derick Heathcoat
Amory became our local Member of Parliament and ended up as
Chancellor of the Exchequer under Harold Macmillan and later became
a viscount. People said that he nearly became Prime Minister himself,
but I don't think he had that look about him. He was very kind to me and
once took me around the House of Commons.

My dreams of a musical career seemed blighted when I went to
work in the factory, but Ron was determined and got in touch with the
London College of Music. It was regarded as the poor man's college, the
major ones being the Royal Academy of Music and the Royal College of
Music, followed by the Guild, which was also very fine. The people at the
London College told Ron that one of the staff would be visiting Exeter
to audition people. Ron took me to play to him and I was invited to the
College for an interview and offered a full scholarship. But I couldn't take
it up and move to London, I just couldn't.

At the same time as he was teaching me, Ron gathered together a group
of boys who could play musical instruments and we all started playing
together.[4] Derick Heathcoat Amory took an interest, suggested that we call
ourselves the Tiverton Youth Orchestra and became our patron. When I
was offered the place at the London College of Music, Ron talked to Derick
Heathcoat Amory about it and the upshot was that the factory covered the
cost of my going up to the College one day a week for tuition. I was given
£2 10s a week for the train fare, food (I always had lunch at Littlewoods)
and overnight accommodation, which Ron arranged for me with friends
he had met on holiday. I would collect the cash from the office on Tuesday,
get an early train on Wednesday morning and return late on Thursday.
I was an anomaly in the factory and inevitably there was some jealousy
about this arrangement. People would say to me, 'You'll be nothing!' They
knew that they were stuck in the factory for life, whereas music offered me
an escape route to another world.

Sir John and Lady Heathcoat Amory were incredibly kind to me and
took a great interest in my progress. Lady Amory loved golf and music
and was actually a British open golf champion. I used to go to their
house sometimes, a massive mansion, and give little concerts to thank
them for their generosity. There was never any pressure to pay back the
money.

My teacher at the College was Angel Grande,[5] a great friend of the Queen of Spain and of Pablo Casals. Like Casals, he was on Franco's blacklist, I think, but unlike him, he was a royalist, whereas Casals was a republican. Grande was a fascinating man, a strong Catholic and a brilliant violinist and fine conductor – the star teacher at the College. I liked him and felt very fortunate. He only had two pupils, so I got lots of attention with lessons always going well over the hour.

Ron badgered me to persuade Grande to play in Tiverton with the Youth Orchestra, and Grande agreed. By the time it was arranged, I was in the army but I managed to get leave to be there. Ron picked me up at the station and I noticed that he had posters all over town advertising the concert. To my horror, he had spelt Grande's name 'Angle' not 'Angel'. 'Oh bugger', said Ron. 'I'll take care of that.' And he did. He went around with a paintbrush, covered over the last two letters and redid them. This was December 1948, the first of the Tiverton Youth Orchestra's celebrity concerts. Years later, I was the celebrity soloist myself on several occasions, the last in 1999 when Ron retired.

National Service

After about a year and a half at the College, I went into the army as a gunner in the Royal Tank Regiment. No one escaped National Service at that time, though you could defer for a couple of years. I discussed it with Angel Grande and he suggested that I get it over with and then go back to College. It was sound advice. When I received the papers saying that I was registered for the army, I went and a lot of it was OK, but I missed my family and Ron terribly. We all wrote lots, and every Saturday I rang Ron in Tiverton. We were stationed at Catterick, in North Yorkshire – beautiful country.

When you go into the army, you learn to kill people. That's what it's for. Those ads showing people learning a trade and doing marvellous things are a joke. When I first got there, I asked the sergeant major if I could go into the band because I was a musician, but he said, 'No, you've come here to learn to fight', and they taught me to fire a gun.

My father was terribly anxious about my being a gunner and he was right; I was hopeless. At the end of three months, we were told that we would get two weeks leave and then be sent to Germany. I was horrified, as I had heard that Germany was a crazy place, divided into sectors with a lot of tension. When the military police arrived to inspect our group, an officer noticed the violin in my cupboard. He asked, if I was musical why wasn't I in the band? I said that I'd tried. He immediately put me in touch with the bandmaster, who told me to report to him and not my regiment when I got back from leave. It was a miracle, because inspections usually consisted of officers walking through the barracks without looking at much, let alone asking questions.

Back from leave, I got a note from the Commander of the Tank Regiment saying, 'Martin, you haven't passed your test as a gunner'. I protested that I was about to join the band. He said that unless I passed, I could be called back to the regiment and maybe not get out of the army. So this sergeant major tested me and I was hopeless, absolutely hopeless, but he passed me on everything; he didn't care. One test was reassembling a Bren gun. It was quite a big thing and you had to lie behind it on your belly. So I put all these bits together and said, 'There you are, sergeant!' He lent over and touched it with his foot and the gun fell to bits. 'Do you think you're going to kill anyone with that?', he asked and ticked 'pass'. 'Can I go back to the band now?' I asked. 'Get out of here' he growled.

There were no string instruments in the band, only brass and woodwind. The bandmaster gave me two weeks to learn the French horn before turning in with the band. I managed with a great deal of help from the first horn player, Peter Clack. Peter was from Swindon and a couple of years older than me. He became my greatest friend in England.

And so I spent the rest of my two years of National Service in the Royal Tank Regiment Band. When the time came to leave, the bandmaster told me that he was putting my name down for Kneller Hall, the army equivalent of the Royal College of Music. Peter had been there; it was a brilliant training ground. That's where all the army bandmasters come from. When I told Peter, he was alarmed. 'Mucker, don't you dare sign anything', he said. 'You're leaving the army. You're not staying here with me. Just say 'No'. Peter had joined up as a teenager, as there were so few opportunities after the war. He won all the prizes but he hated the army.

The bandmaster put huge pressure on me, saying how well the army looked after you. 'Anyone can play the violin', he said. 'There are hundreds of them out there, whereas you'd have a great future in the army, you'd be looked after.' But I stuck to my guns and took advantage of the army scheme to help people finishing National Service to get into tertiary institutions. It was a way of getting in by the back door but you had to be good enough. I applied to the Royal College of Music.

On the day of my audition, I remember walking down Prince Consort Road and almost knocking myself out walking into a lamp-post. I was early and hoped to be able to rest a bit and recover. My face was scarlet, my head ached and I had a huge bump on my head. But the commissioner sent me straight up. Alexander Gibson, the marvellous Scottish conductor, accompanied me on the piano – I think it was Mozart – and I got in.

Peter told me that if I hadn't left the Army, he would never have spoken to me again. He himself eventually got permission to leave and went on to play with all the main London orchestras, including the Philharmonic, and became Head of Brass at Charterhouse School.

At the Royal College

The Royal College of Music is in a beautiful part of London, opposite the Albert Hall. Ron Davey took me to see it on our first visit to the city. 'That's where you want to be, Chris', he said. The London College of Music didn't have the same prestige but there was no way at that time that I could have gone to the Royal College. Ron was thrilled for me when I actually did get in and would be studying under some of the world's finest musicians. I was there for three wonderfully happy years.

When I arrived, I needed a better violin and someone told me about an old lady who would be prepared to lend me one. It was a gorgeous violin and she was hoping to sell it for £500 – a huge amount of money then. It was an unusual instrument, a beautiful orangey colour and decorative without being fussy, and it had obviously been made for a wealthy patron. The old lady thought that if it was used, people would see it and word would get out. She called me 'Mr Martin' and assumed that I was part of the David Martin Quartet, well known in London at the time. I didn't disillusion her. She was completely nuts and when no buyer was forthcoming she suggested that I throw the violin under a bus so she could collect the insurance money. She gave it to Sotheby's to sell at auction, and when it reached £450 she bid herself to push up the price. They made her pay the commission and she wasn't allowed to put the violin back in the auction for another twelve months. I think she sold it privately in the end.

At my interview with the Royal College, I had been asked who I wanted to study with. The great Albert Sammons was like a god to me – he was probably the most famous English violinist ever – so I asked for him.[6] They told me that Mr Sammons was getting old, had terrible arthritis and was very selective with his pupils. He only had three at that stage: Tessa Robins, Hugh Bean, who became the leader of the Philharmonia, and Alan Loveday, a New Zealander who performed with St Martin-in-the-Fields. They put me with Marie Wilson, who was co-leader of the BBC Orchestra and a fine musician, but I was disappointed as the next big figure at the College after Sammons was the Danish violinist, Henry Holst – no relation to Gustav. He had been leader of the Berlin Philharmonic in his twenties, was a well-known solo performer in the 1940s and taught at the Royal College for years.[7] At the end of my first year, I did transfer to him and Marie was lovely about it. She understood.

When Marie was teaching me, there were a couple of times she couldn't make the class and she told me that she was sending someone else to take me. 'You'll like him', she said. 'His name is Neville Marriner and he's a fine player.'[8] She was right; I liked him a lot. He wasn't much older than me and was very funny. When he asked what I was playing and I said Paganini, he asked, 'Haven't you got something easier?' So I dug out some Bach.

During my time at the Royal College, I had a girlfriend called Una George, a violin player and my first real love. I had met her at the London College and we corresponded for the two years when I was in the army. She was teaching in north London while I was at the Royal College. She was a good teacher but never a great player. We stayed in touch after I left London and she married someone else. Many years later, when I was living in Melbourne, my mother wrote to me to tell me that Una had died. She knew I would be very upset. The extraordinary thing is that by the same post there was a little parcel from Una with a book of Mozart scores and a letter. 'Do you remember playing this music?', she wrote. My mother's letter came by air and Una's package by sea, yet they arrived on the same day.

Concerts in London were always very affordable, even the best, and one evening I went to hear a recital by Isaac Stern. The next day Henry Holst raved about it, saying how wonderful Stern was. A few months later, Jascha Heifetz gave a concert in London. He played the Walton Violin Concerto, which was written for him, and the Mendelssohn Violin Concerto. It was an amazing evening. I've never seen so many violinists in the audience. At my lesson that week, Holst asked if I'd heard Heifetz and raved about him, too. I reminded him what he'd said about Stern and he said, 'Forget Stern! Heifetz is the man!' Stern was wiped. Szymon Goldberg used to say the same, that to violinists there was never anyone but Heifetz. He is certainly the most impressive player I have heard in my life. Nobody plays the violin remotely like him – his craft, his colour, it's all a miracle. It's not to say that he is the greatest musician or the greatest artist – just the greatest violinist.

I once heard a series of radio talks on the ABC [Australian Broadcasting Commission] called 'The Greatest Violinists'. I thought that the presenter made a mistake in presenting recordings of Heifetz playing pieces by Sibelius and Tchaikovsky, because there are many recordings of these that are equally good. No one owns great music like the concertos of Beethoven, Mozart or Tchaikovsky. When the violinist is playing it – whether it be Oistrakh or Perlman or anybody of that ilk – for that moment the music belongs to them, but just for that moment.

Heifetz, however, played a lot of small, even trite, pieces that you would think are nothing much, but he put so much colour and interest in them – nobody owns them as he does. Think of the *Hora staccato*.[9] He took it for himself after he heard the composer play it and performed it with such style. He was never vulgar, whereas when Isaac Stern played it he put in these terrible slides. Yehudi did the same.

With players like Stern and Yehudi, the greater the music, the greater their respect for the music and therefore the greater the performance. They are never vulgar with big pieces, but Heifetz gave the small pieces the same dignity and attention that he paid the greatest pieces. I think Pablo Casals was the same with the cello. One of my favourite Heifetz pieces is his recording of *Berceuse* with Bing Crosby.[10] The playing is superb. What a pity that the ABC didn't play this or one of the many other small pieces recorded by Heifetz, such as *Estrellita* – a beautiful little piece, which, if you play it in G major, is terribly easy. It has an open string and a nice harmonic. So what did Heifetz do? He played it down a semi-tone in F sharp major, which meant that he could paint his own colour on every sound with no open strings.

Orchestras were always short of viola players, so the College was keen to encourage more people to take it up. I wanted to do piano as a second instrument, but they said that if you can play violin well, you can play the viola and they offered to find me an instrument. Cecil Aronowitz taught me.[11] Cecil was Jewish South African, famous in London for his chamber music. He was with the Amadeus Quartet for years and years. We became close friends and he was enormously helpful to me. Where Holst was great technically, Cecil was musical. He had the most natural way of playing the viola that I have ever seen. He played pieces such as the *Marin Marais* dances and the Brahms E Flat Sonata with enormous charm but didn't like to stretch himself technically.

Cecil, too, started with the violin and had actually studied with Henry Holst. We were both violinists in feeling, and in fact I never lost my love for the fiddle because the repertoire stretches forever in comparison with the viola. When I was working with Cecil, he didn't like to think of my studying the violin with Holst and Holst didn't like me doing viola with Cecil. They got on well but that was uncomfortable for me.

The viola which the College lent me was a monster, a big ugly instrument, but it made quite a good sound. We never played scales or studies in our lessons, just pieces. Cecil also coached a quartet that I formed in College and was marvellous with that. He had an uncanny ear for chamber music and insisted that what you played had to be heard. He once said to me, 'Chris, what are you doing? You have a long note.' 'But my part there is not important', I told him. 'The composer put it there because he wants to hear it', he said. I believe he's right. Every part needs to be heard and understood. Suppose you are an amateur musician playing second violin, and you go to hear a professional quartet. You should be able to hear the second violin all the time, otherwise there's no point in the second violin's being there. The best composers wrote in that way. Not all, by any means. Some quartets are flooded with sound, but the great composers – Mozart, Beethoven – have that balance.

Cecil was the loveliest man you could ever meet and everyone was amazed that he waited until he was forty before he married. He had a very sweet tooth, taking five sugars in his tea and always eating cakes. He also smoked endlessly. I never smoked, myself. People said that I would start smoking when I did my National Service, because everyone smoked in the services, but I didn't. I thought it a disgusting habit. Cigarettes were rationed and I used to give my rations away.

The degree course at the Royal College lasted three years, at the end of which you took your ARCM (Associate of the Royal College of Music). For some reason, Henry Holst was on the panel when I went for my final exam. He shouldn't have been, as he was my teacher; it was a conflict of interest. As it happens, I had changed a lot of things that he had given me and I could see that he was annoyed by this. He cross-questioned me about it later, demanding to know why I had made the changes. What could I say? I didn't get my degree and think it was him who failed me. Not having a degree never made any difference to me, but my mother was sad that I didn't have a certificate to put on the wall.

Around this time, I was doing a fair amount of freelance playing as well as playing a lot of chamber music. One of the quartets I played in was at a wonderful house in the middle of London, owned by Lady Wilson, who played the cello rather poorly. Béla Bartók had stayed there and she used to say what a sweet man he was.[12] I wondered at this. If you saw a photo of Bartók, you would never think of him as a sweet man. She showed me a little cello piece that he wrote for her on a sheet of paper signed 'with affection'. Years later, when I was at the University of Melbourne, I met a Bartók scholar and told him this story. He tried to track that paper down, getting friends in London who knew the family to search for it, but they never found it. Presumably when Lady Wilson died, somebody picked up a stack of papers thinking that they weren't important and threw them out.

In your last year at college, you had to start thinking about work. I was lucky as the factory continued to give me the £2 10s a week while I studied. My parents couldn't do anything for me; they had nothing. I organised a couple of auditions, one with the BBC [British Broadcasting Commission] and the other with Sadlers Wells. Cecil wanted me to audition on the viola not the violin, but I wasn't too sure about it because in those days the BBC gave you a frightful sight-reading test. Now every orchestra in the world will give you notes from pieces that you might play and you have a chance to practise them; that's a big part of the audition. At the BBC audition, I played my prepared pieces well and felt good about them. Then they gave me the sight-reading. It was a piece of Wagner – a handwritten manuscript, completely illegible, with a fast tempo – two, three, four and off you go.

I went like a lunatic and, when it was over, one of the panel – the orchestra conductor – stood up and said, 'Please look at line three. What do you see there?' I looked, 'Oh, it changes clef'. 'You didn't seem to notice', he said. Then, 'Would you look at line seven; it changes key there, doesn't it?' On and on it went. I didn't get that job. Had I played the violin, I would have done much better. I didn't have enough experience with the viola. The Sadlers Wells position didn't work out either, as the fellow who was leaving decided to stay.

Following that, I had two more auditions: one for the Yorkshire Symphony Orchestra and the other for the Liverpool Philharmonic. They were for violin, as I decided not to risk the viola or I might never get a job. I was offered both. Liverpool appealed to me more, but before taking up the job my friend Joan Dickson invited me to play in a quartet at her home in London[13] and told me that the New Edinburgh String Quartet was being formed. The Australian violinist Robert Cooper was first violin,[14] his wife Anne, a beautiful red-headed Scot, was second violin and Joan was cello. Joan said that she'd love me to join the quartet but would have to ask Robert and Anne.

When the Coopers heard me play at their flat in London, they asked me to join them and I said that I would love to, as I had always wanted the experience of playing with a professional quartet. The next question was, 'When can you start?' Now I was in a bind. I told Bob Cooper that I had already accepted Liverpool, so he said to go for a few months and then to leave. So I did. It was 1953 and I was twenty-three.

Auditioning for a quartet is not easy. You have to see if you fit musically and personally with the other players and demonstrate the potential for developing with the group. Total musical empathy in a quartet takes time, but you have to show that it's going to come, that you will fit together. It took me all of my six years with the New Edinburgh Quartet to gain the experience to be able to play quartets all my life.

The Musicians Union, which formed in Liverpool, was against my joining the orchestra without a contract from the start, rather than the usual trial period followed by the offer of a contract. But a trial period suited me well, because I knew that I would be leaving. After a couple of weeks, Hugo Rignold called me in and told me that he loved my work and offered me a permanent contract. Hugo had taken over from Sir Malcolm Sargent a few years before and was a superb musician. I had to tell him about Edinburgh. He was very nice about it, and wished me luck, even though the orchestra wanted me to stay.

The Edinburgh experience

Joan Dickson invited me to stay with her in Edinburgh while I found my feet. She lived with her parents in a beautiful house in Doune Terrace, Newtown – a very high-class area, very different from my digs in London. All the time I had been studying at the Royal College, I had been living with a Mr and Mrs Parent, who were poor as anything and lived in a tiny, horrible little house in Harringay. Mrs Parent was a lovely woman and looked after me so well. Their name was pronounced the French way, because her husband was French Canadian. He had been on merchant ships during the war, was sunk twice but lived to tell the tale. He was a tough, hard man with a good heart. Sometimes Mrs Parent would be away for the night looking after the children of a rich family whom she worked for. Because he wasn't normally allowed to drink when his wife was there, Mr Parent would get completely and utterly plastered and I would come home to find him lying on the floor.

Living with the Dicksons in Doune Terrace was an incredible contrast. Joan's father was a lawyer, a very good one, a senior partner in his firm. I liked him very much. Her mother was strict Scottish and informed me that I was a paying guest and had to watch my ps and qs. The cook, Mrs McGuiness, made a delicious meal every night. One evening, we had chicken. When I picked up a drumstick, Joan's mother said, 'Christopher! We don't touch chicken bones. Only game birds, Christopher, only game birds.' And sure enough, a little bit later we had pheasant and I was allowed to pick up the tiny bones and chew.

Joan had a sister, Hester, who was a wonderful pianist as well as playing viola in the orchestra. While I was staying with the Dicksons, I fell in love with Hester.[15] She was about thirty and had just lost her husband. She wasn't living in the house and we didn't actually have an affair, just saw a lot of each other. I thought that it was our secret, absolutely, but I soon realised that her mother was very put out by our friendship, though she didn't say anything. The last time I saw Hester was when I went to Edinburgh with the Chamber Strings of Melbourne in 2009. Our friendship has lasted a lifetime.

Hester's godfather was the marvellous conductor, Sir Adrian Boult.[16] He came to stay occasionally, always very charming, very much the English gentleman. The Dicksons knew a lot of interesting people but among the most extraordinary of their friends were the Hungarian d'Arányi sisters, Jelly and Adila.[17] They were great-nieces of Joseph Joachim, one of the greatest violinists of the nineteenth century. The d'Arányi sisters were extremely well known, particularly in the 1920s and 1930s. Both Bartók and Arthur Somervell dedicated violin sonatas to Adila, while Vaughan Williams called Jelly his ninth muse and wrote a concerto for her. Ravel's *Tzigane* (meaning 'gipsy'), possibly his finest work, was written for Jelly. When I met her, she said, 'I am Tzigane!', with her eyes flashing. She was quite a character.

They both settled in London and Adila married a barrister called Alexandre Fachiri, but the two sisters always did a lot together – their lives were closely intertwined. They came to stay with the Dicksons when I was living with them, and I found them fascinating. I once asked Jelly if the story of her finding a lost Schumann concerto was true. 'Of course, darlink!', she said.

Adila actually told me the story, though I knew something of it already and that it was widely regarded as hogwash. Adila said that she and Jelly used to go to séances in London and on one occasion Schumann appeared and asked Jelly why she didn't play his violin concerto. 'But there isn't one', she protested. 'Yes there is', he said. 'It's in the Hochschule in Berlin and I want you to play it.' It was 1938 and she was Jewish, but she went to Berlin to find the concerto, although they told her at the Hochschule that it didn't exist. Apparently she went to another séance and Schumann appeared again and insisted that his concerto was there. So she went back and made a big fuss. She was a powerful and courageous artist, so they agreed to go through their old records and, sure enough, they found the piece.

It was almost Schumann's last work and had been written when he was very ill. The violin part was finished but the orchestration was sketchy, so the Hochschule commissioned Paul Hindemith to make it playable. Jelly desperately wanted to be the first to play it in public, but they objected: 'A Jew playing Schumann, a German composer?' Georg Kulenkampff, a top German violinist who wasn't opposed to the Nazis, was asked to play it. Once it had been performed in public, it was available for other musicians and Yehudi Menuhin heard about it and said that he wanted to play it. He was very young at the time and in America. Jelly in the meantime was trying to organise a concert with Sir Adrian Boult and they fixed a date, but Yehudi got in first and recorded the piece. It's not a great work but it has some exquisite moments and Yehudi's recording is beautiful. Jelly finally got to do the third performance in London.

The story about the séance was well known in music circles and regarded as a load of rubbish, but how else could Jelly have found that piece when she had no idea it existed? Adila told me that the story was absolutely true. Hester often accompanied Jelly and Adila when they were staying in Doune Terrace and told me that once, when she was rehearsing the Schumann with Jelly, Adila asked her sister why she had changed the bowing for a certain section. 'Because Robert told me to', she said.

The New Edinburgh Quartet was formed by the Music Department of Edinburgh University to give a series of concerts during the year and also to play in the university orchestra, which wasn't very strong. It worked out well. We didn't get a big salary – more of a retainer – but there were lots of opportunities for us as freelance musicians, lots of music clubs, lots of concerts. The quartet played often in northern England and Scotland, travelled in Europe and performed in three Edinburgh Festivals. At one Festival, we played a quintet with the great Hungarian pianist Ernő Dohnányi, then living in New York.[18]

Dohnányi was one of the greatest pianists of the time, known for his phenomenal memory. He was also a successful composer. On the day of our first rehearsal, the four of us were sitting waiting for him in the Usher Hall when in walked this tiny man. 'Good morning, have you got the music?', he said. After telling us that he hadn't looked at it for twenty-five years, he sat down, opened the first page and proceeded to play the whole work from memory. He didn't look at the music at all. I have never heard anything like his playing – the colours he produced; it was amazing. When we had finished our rehearsal, we asked if he wanted to take the music with him and he said, no, he didn't need it.

My first experience of conducting was in Edinburgh. I had a lot of friends who were professional and amateur musicians, and somebody suggested that we start a small string orchestra with me conducting. 'I haven't done any conducting', I protested. 'But you know all about strings, you can do it', they said, and they were right. I found that conducting strings came naturally to me. We called it the Christopher Martin Chamber Orchestra and gave a lot of concerts, many of them at Reid Hall in Edinburgh University. We had a lot of good soloists – singers, pianists, violinists – and we also had a lot of fun. The Reid Hall is a fine venue. I played again there years later with the Chamber Strings of Melbourne, on one of our tours. To my surprise, the Christopher Martin Orchestra kept going for about twenty years after I left Edinburgh. It expanded to include professionals from London – conductors and players – and kept my name, always sending me copies of their programmes until it stopped.

Playing for J.B. Priestley

The novelist J.B. Priestley knew Joan Dickson well and actually mentions her in his book *Delight*. He used to play chamber music for fun, but Joan said that he was a dreadful pianist who played badly – but then she was a professional. He lived on the Isle of Wight with his wife, Jacquetta Hawkes, the famous archaeologist. Theirs was a large house with a wide hall and grand staircase and they used to hold concerts there. People came from all over the island and sat on the stairs or in the hall – there was plenty of room. The New Edinburgh Quartet went several times and stayed the weekend, once with the pianist Eric Harrison and another time with Leon Goossens, the finest oboe player in England at the time.

During the concerts, J.B. Priestley retreated to a tiny room off the hallway, probably a smoking room. He sat in the dark with the door open, a full bottle of whiskey and a tumbler on a table in front of him, smoking his pipe. He was in heaven.

I've performed in a number of beautiful homes, even castles, including 'Glamis', the Scottish home of the late Queen Mother, though she wasn't there at the time. One of the most distinguished private audiences I've played to was at Holyrood Palace in Edinburgh. It was quite an auspicious occasion and we played the Schubert Quartet in G Major sitting in front of this magnificent van Dyck painting of Charles I on a horse. What a setting for Schubert's greatest quartet! Afterwards there was a fantastic reception and we were introduced to the Prime Minister, Harold Macmillan.

I remember chatting to a lady-in-waiting, so there must have been members of the royal family there too. She was very pretty and we were getting on famously when I was told Anthony Asquith had asked to be introduced to me. Even though he was hugely famous, I left the lady-in-waiting reluctantly. Anthony Asquith wanted to talk about the music – especially the last movement, which he said always killed him. He went on and on about the clash between the major and minor chords and I thought he was going to fall over he was so excited about them. Eventually I got back to the lady-in-waiting. 'Did you get offered a part in a film?' she asked me. 'No', I said. 'He only wanted to talk about the B flat.'

The Edinburgh Quartet was going wonderfully well until Joan Dickson left. We found a replacement for her in Ian Hampton, who had been a student of Joan's. His father was the noted cellist Colin Hampton, who played with the Griller Quartet.[19] Anne Cooper and Ian Hampton fell passionately in love and this meant the end of the quartet. Bob realised what was going on and was angry, though I never noticed a thing until Anne told me herself. Bob decided to go back to London, where he had a lot of work commitments, and then to return to Australia. Ian also went off to work in London. I remember Anne and I looking at each other and wondering what to do. She said, 'We can't stay in Edinburgh now, there's nothing to stay for'. We knew the Netherlands Chamber Orchestra was auditioning in London and she said, 'Let's go for it!' So we auditioned and were both offered places. In Edinburgh, they asked me to stay on and form another quartet but I felt that I couldn't start again with a new group even though I really loved Edinburgh. Ian went back and joined the newly formed Edinburgh Quartet.

Anne and I left Edinburgh at the same time. It was 1959 and people thought we had run off together but it wasn't me she loved, it was Ian. Their affair continued for years but he eventually married someone else. I don't think that Anne ever got over him. Back in Australia, Bob led the orchestra in Adelaide for many years before going to Perth to lead the orchestra there and eventually retire.

Music and marriage in Holland

The Netherlands Chamber Orchestra was conducted by Szymon Goldberg, who at seventeen had been the youngest leader of the Berlin Philharmonic under Furtwängler.[20] The orchestra did some fantastic tours – to Greece, Israel, America, Japan, France and Germany. What a time! But Szymon never came with us to Germany. He was Jewish and had been kicked out by Goebbels just before the war and couldn't bring himself to set foot in the country again, even though they begged him to come. Members of his family died in the camps. We had guest conductors instead and Benjamin Britten was one. He came over to do a concert with Peter Pears and Barry Tuckwell, the Australian horn player who took the place of Dennis Brain when he died.[21]

Dennis was a great musician and Ben always used him whenever he did anything with the horn. Dennis loved cars and would drive at high speed from Edinburgh to London overnight in his Triumph TR2. One night after playing with Eugene Ormandy and the Philadelphia Orchestra at the Edinburgh Festival, he asked if anyone wanted to go with him to London. He was due to make a recording the next morning. There were no takers, so he went on his own and tragically was killed on the road.

In Holland, they called Ben 'Meneer Britten' and he accepted that. The Dutch, like the Germans, are very formal. When he saw me, he cried, 'It's Christopher!' To the horror of the Dutch, I said, 'Hello, Ben'. They couldn't believe that a mere player in the orchestra could address a guest conductor by his first name.

When Goldberg took the orchestra to Japan, I was surprised considering what a rough time he must have had at the hands of the Japanese during the war. Sitting next to him on the bus one day, I asked him why he was prepared to go to Japan but not Germany. He said that, to him, the oriental mindset was different and he did not feel the same animosity towards the Japanese. He said Berlin before the war was the most cultured, civilised, vibrant, musical place in the world. He found it incredible that the city could degenerate the way it did under the Nazis and would never set foot in Germany again.

The orchestra travelled a lot, including in Israel and America. The Israeli tour was amazing. We spent about ten days there and gave some wonderful concerts. Some of that time we stayed on a kibbutz not far from the Syrian border. It was before the 1967 war and occasionally a Syrian soldier would take a pot-shot at an Israeli and we were warned about walking in particular areas. One evening, in the middle of a Mozart concert, the lights went out and the place went black. Nobody stopped. We knew those pieces so well that we all went on playing. We couldn't see Goldberg, of course, but he started to snap his fingers in time to the rhythm – snap, snap, snap. The lights were out for quite a while.

I have never seen Goldberg so happy as he was in Israel. The reason was that he met up with a brother whom he had last seen in Poland before the war. He came from a big family – eleven children, I think – and this was his only surviving sibling. It was very touching how he found him there.

Goldberg was very kind to Anne. Ian went to live in Canada and I don't think she ever stopped loving him. Even though she was a terribly attractive woman, she never married again. She stayed with the orchestra for some time and then went to Berkeley in California, where she set up the Anne Crowden Music School for strings. It became famous not only in America but around the world. I often saw articles written about it and how successful Anne's students were.

Some amazing soloists played with us in the Netherlands, including the great Hungarian pianists Annie Fischer and Lily Kraus. Elisabeth Schwarzkopf sang with us a few times, as did Victoria de los Angeles and the wonderful Teresa Berganza whom I adored. More women than men performed with us, but I don't know why. Perhaps because most of the string solo work was done by Goldberg himself. He both conducted and played, as Richard Tognetti does here in Australia.

The leader of the orchestra was another Hungarian, Tomas Magyar. He was thick from the neck up, really thick. He and Goldberg didn't get on. They used to play the Bach double together but it was something of a travesty. Tomas was marvellous, he could play anything and his command of the violin was technically more than equal to Goldberg's. As well, he was a nice man but he had no brains. I think he got the job of leader because he had lived in Holland a long time and had Dutch citizenship. Naturally, the orchestra had a lot of foreigners including several English people, one American and a number of players from other parts of Europe. But the Dutch are very particular about their own, and if there was a position vacant they would insist on giving it to a Dutch person if there was one available. The bloke sitting next to Tomas was Dutch and he was thick, too.

On one of our tours to Germany, Ben Britten was guest conductor and spent a week rehearsing with us before we left Holland. One of the pieces we played was his *Variations on a Theme of Frank Bridge*. The leading violin has a solo – just a quick run, written in single notes – and Tomas being Tomas did fingered octaves. It's a virtuoso thing that some people do, and not easy, so you have to be good. Tomas kept looking at Britten for approval but Ben didn't give away anything. After our third rehearsal Tomas couldn't stand it any more and said, 'Meneer Britten, do you like fingered octaves?' And Ben said, 'I think we'll leave it as I wrote it'. It was like – squash! I felt sorry for Tomas; he was so eager to please.

Tomas's brother Gabor was a famous cellist who had a successful career as a soloist before taking over from Vilmos Palotai in the Hungarian String Quartet, whose work was so great that people went specifically to hear him. Gabor became the cellist in 1956. He was a wonderful player but not the same stature as Palotai.

My fate was sealed when I met Annette. Her sister Gill Rosefield had studied with Goldberg and played violin in the Netherlands Orchestra with me. She mentioned to me that Annette was coming to see her in Holland, that she was a cellist and we could play some quartet music together. Gill had a photograph of Annette and when I saw it I knew that I had to meet her. She was as beautiful as I expected. After the first time we played together, Gill asked Annette what she thought of me. Evidently Annette said that I was impossible, unbearable. I think I was showing off and trying to make an impression, and it backfired.

Within a week of that meeting, the orchestra was going to Aix-en-Provence to play in the music festival. Gill invited Annette to come and somehow we just clicked. We explored the town so familiar from the paintings of Cezanne and fell in love. We were in Marseilles when we got engaged and I bought Annette a ring. It all just happened so quickly.

The orchestra was about to go on a big tour and Annette was heading for Israel. Her grandfather was Russian and her mother of Irish-Spanish descent, but she is one hundred per cent Jewish. While she was away, she had second thoughts about marrying me and asked herself what on earth she thought she was doing agreeing to marry someone after such a short time. She felt that it was because the circumstances of our meeting were so marvellous, the atmosphere so magical. On her return to Paris, she wrote me a letter saying that she thought her life didn't include me. No sooner had she posted it than she regretted it. Just like her to change her mind! She waited for hours in the freezing cold for the postman to come and empty the box. When he did, she insisted on having her letter back. He was horrified. 'Madame, Madame, I can't give it to you. I can't!' Annette wept. 'I'm in love', she told him. 'I broke it off'. His heart melted, of course. She was a very beautiful woman.

We met again in London and went on holiday together in a funny little hotel in Falmouth, in Cornwall, and while we were there we decided to get married. My old girlfriend Una George and her husband were our only witnesses. I rang my mother and said, 'Mum, I'm going to get married, do you want to come?' She said, 'No, I can't. You carry on.' 'OK, Mum', I said, 'sorry about that. We'll be in touch.' And so there we were, married. We looked at each other after the ceremony and wondered what we'd done.

Annette: My first love was ballet – an obsession – but my build was not right and my cello was waiting for me. I played trios with my sisters – Gill on the violin and Fay on the piano. We lived in Brighton, Melbourne; it was stifling. I used to wonder – where is the world? I would look across the bay to Williamstown and imagine that it was Europe – but it wasn't. If people wanted to make things happen, they had to do it themselves – like Mischa Kogan who started the Soirées Musicales, chamber music played initially in private houses and then in Coppin Hall in Punt Road in Prahran. The concerts were on a Sunday night and were exciting in the extreme.

Like everyone else I knew, I eventually went to London in the late 1950s and arrived in the worst winter – yellow headlights at three in the afternoon and my nose always dirty. There was a bus strike and people went around with purple faces and two pairs of gloves and never complained. So I took a plane to Paris and looked up Paul Tortelier in the phone book. I had heard him play at the Albert Hall. He was wonderful. He answered the phone and I told him that I was a cellist from Australia and he invited me to see his class and I played for him. He encouraged me to enter the Paris Conservatoire. I took the exams but made myself sick with nerves and didn't get in.

After three years in Paris, I decided to go and live in Israel. Before leaving, I went to see my sister Gill who was on tour with the Netherlands Orchestra in the south of France. That's where I had the romantic meeting with Chris. We only had a few weeks before he was leaving for America on tour and I was going to Israel, so we got engaged and bought a ring. In Haifa, I felt completely at home and joined a couple of orchestras. I seriously thought of staying on but Gill wrote to me saying, 'What are you doing ? Chris is waiting for you.' So I went back, though I hardly remembered what he looked like. We didn't really know what we were doing when we got married, but music was always our great bond and here we are fifty years later, still friends. We have weathered an awful lot.

Christopher Martin at the start of his career as a professional musician.
Photo: John Vickers.

Above & below
Chris's parents, Frank and
Sarah Martin, at the time
of their marriage.

Christopher John Martin, aged three.

Ron Davey in about 1950 playing his beautiful eighteenth-century
Lorenzo Storioni violin.

The Tiverton Youth Orchestra at the Heathcoat Hall in Tiverton in December 1948, with Angel Grande (standing far left) as guest soloist. Chris Martin, concertmaster (seated), and Ron Davey on the left holding the baton.

Peter Clack (far left) and Christopher Martin (second left) playing the
French horn in the Army band.

Christopher Martin and his first girlfriend, Una George,
on the beach in Cornwall.

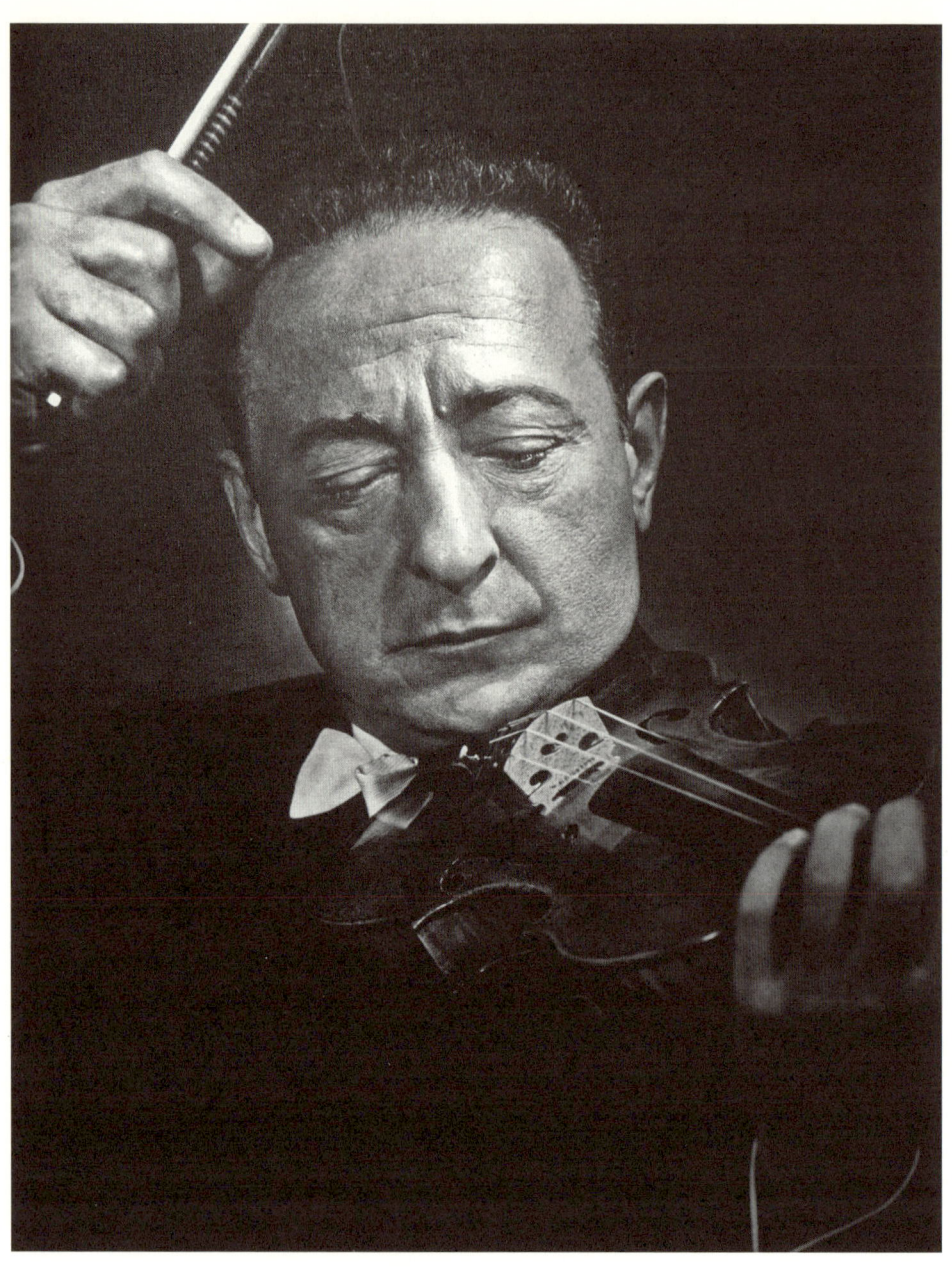

Jascha Heifetz, the violinist's violinist, c. 1950s.
Yousuf Karsh, *Portraits of Greatness*, Thomas Nelson & Sons, 1960.

The New Edinburgh String Quartet after the departure of Joan Dickson, with Robert Cooper, first violin, his wife Anne Crowden, second violin, Christopher Martin, viola and Ian Hampton, cello. Photo: John Vickers.

Above Members of the Netherlands Chamber Orchestra travelling to New York on the SS *Rotterdam*. From left to right: Mrs Goldberg, Keas van Hoving, Alec Mayhew, Mary de Light and husband Ben, Szymon Goldberg, Chris Martin and Gillian Rosefield.

Below Chris and Annette at the captain's cocktail party on the SS *Rotterdam* on the way to New York. Photos: Gillian Rosefield.

The Netherlands Chamber Orchestra arriving in New York at the start of their 1960 tour. Szymon Goldberg is in the front on the left, Chris is in the middle of the second row, and Gillian Rosefield is third from the right in the back.

Chris and Annette falling in love in Aix-en-Provence.

Mrs Parent, pronounced Par-*ent*, Chris's landlady in London. He took Annette to stay with her after Chris and Annette married, and Annette was moved by Mrs Parent's affection for Chris but astonished at how uncomfortable the bed was.

Chris and Annette soon after arriving in Melbourne. The photograph was taken by violen teacher Nathan Gutman, a friend of the Rosefield family.

Annette and Chris created quite a stir in Melbourne as a young, talented and glamorous couple. Photo: *Herald Sun*.

The Paul McDermott String Quartet with Paul McDermott, first violin, Alex Burlakov, second violin, and Henry Wenig, cello. Chris, viola, had fallen in the park and broken his leg.

Australia

At first we stayed on in Holland, playing in different orchestras, but under pressure from Annette's mother, we left for Australia within a year. It was 1963. The hardest thing was saying goodbye to my mother. Ron was fine. 'You have to do it', he said. Coming by boat then took six weeks, because the Suez Canal was closed and so we went around the Cape. Annette's mother paid our fares and it was a wonderful, wonderful trip. When we arrived in Melbourne, Mrs Rosefield took us to this little timber cottage in Gardenvale. Everything was there – furniture and food. It was a charmer of a house – small but beautiful. She said, 'Darlings, it's yours if you want it. If you don't, that's OK.' We burst into tears, we couldn't believe it.

Annette insisted that I learn to drive. The police did the driving test in those days. The first time I took the test, I did the parking bit then I was asked to drive. I started off, got to an intersection, put my hand up as you had to then and went across. There was nobody about as it was early afternoon. The policeman was riding alongside me and my instructor was looking at me so oddly, I could tell that he was dying to tell me something. Suddenly the policeman yelled, 'Pull in, pull in to your left!' Only then did I realise that I was driving on the wrong side of the road.

The next time I took the test, I had a crook policeman. He was rough and started asking me questions before I even got in the car. 'That's wrong', he said. 'I can't pass you.' My instructor was furious because my answers were right. We went into the police station to complain to the sergeant, who prevaricated. 'I'm prepared to take my officer's word against yours', he told me, 'but I'll give you another test as soon as you want one and you won't have to pay for it'.

Before we left London, Annette and I had auditioned for the Melbourne Symphony Orchestra,[22] then called the Victorian Symphony Orchestra, with its chief conductor, Georges Tzipine.[23] He was a funny little Frenchman and a terrific conductor, without being remarkable. He wasn't in the class of Pierre Monteux or Jean Martinon but was very skilled and clear, as the French often are, and we did some difficult works with him. We rehearsed six hours a day, starting at 10 a.m., and Tzipine couldn't bear it because he liked a siesta after lunch. He would often stop at 12.30 p.m. instead of 1p.m. and not start again till 2.30 p.m., which meant that the orchestra was hanging about for two hours. His wife was

Australian and he really wanted to settle here and thought that the job would be there for a very long time. In fact, it wasn't. The orchestra got fed up with him, and his contract wasn't renewed.

In those days, the MSO did an annual concert for the Musicians' Provident Fund and people gave their services for nothing, including whichever conductor was invited to take part. All the money collected went into this fund to look after members of the orchestra if they got sick – like the Musicians' Benevolent Fund in England. It was customary to give the conductor a small gift, and the first time that Tzipine was to conduct the concert the orchestra asked him what he would like. To their horror, he said that he wanted a television set. Televisions were still a novelty then and a decent one cost a lot of money, but they got him one.

The leader of the orchestra, Maurice Clare, started a chamber orchestra within the MSO. Eric Challoner, the viola lead, was a nervous man. At one time we were rehearsing a concert with the English conductor Boyd Neel, who had a fine chamber orchestra in the UK. There was quite a big viola solo in one piece and Eric was fine in rehearsals, but come the concert and I could see that he was a nervous wreck. When the solo part was coming up, he put his viola on his lap and stopped playing. He looked terrified. Boyd looked at me and whispered urgently, 'You play it, you play it!' I had never played it before but I did alright, and after that I always led the viola section. These days, the leader and deputy leader switch solos a lot to give the deputy more experience.

The MSO then didn't compare with the best in England, but was a very good orchestra and had some fine players. A big orchestra has over sixty or seventy people, so you're bound to find people you like, which I did in Melbourne. I met some pretty remarkable people whom I liked a lot. It was fashionable then to talk about Australia's being a backwater but I think that anywhere you go, you will find people who make music. This was certainly true of Melbourne. One such person was Paul McDermott, who founded Music in the Round.[24] Paul had played violin with the Philharmonia in London and was a fine musician. He came back to Australia because he was from a big Catholic family and wanted to bring up his own children here. He invited Annette and me to join the Paul McDermott String Quartet and we were also involved with Music in the Round.

In those days, the ABC controlled the symphony orchestras – which wasn't such a bad thing, because it brought many great artists from Europe, who spent maybe a couple of months in Australia. The ABC made sure that it was worth their while by organising concerts and recitals in every state. They would perform in Melbourne, then Geelong and maybe Bendigo, before going on to Sydney or Perth. Tours were so much more leisurely than today, and it meant that the ABC orchestras benefited from playing with some great guest conductors and performers.

Otto Klemperer came and so did Eugene Ormandy – not in my time, though I did play under an astonishing Belgian conductor, André Cluytens, who conducted the Berlin Philharmonic and under Arvīd Jansons, who became principal conductor of the Hallé Orchestra. Violinist Joseph Suk, Dvořák's grandson, was an absolute delight and there was the marvellous Hungarian violinist, György Pauk, whom we came to know well. We played ensemble music together. He mentioned Goldberg and I asked him if he had had lessons from him. He was upset and shouted at me. 'No, no, I play for him! I no have lessons!' 'Lessons' was the wrong word to use because Pauk could play as well as Goldberg, but the reason that good violinists like him played to Goldberg was for his insights. Goldberg always had something interesting to say about the music. He was also enormously respected for his playing, especially for his Mozart sonatas. His recordings with pianist Lili Kraus – who played with my quartet in Edinburgh – are thought by some to be the best.

Mstislav Rostropovich also came to Australia when I was with the MSO and he gave recitals, as did the Hungarian pianist, Peter Frankl. There were many, many wonderful players and great musicians, though I never really gave much thought to it. If it had been Heifetz – then I would have thought about it! But we did get Isaac Stern.

Stern was doing a concerto with the orchestra and got angry because they couldn't do something he was asking. 'Like this! Like this!', he shouted as he took an agitated up bow. The bow got caught in the strings and its tip snapped. It was a tragedy that you can't believe, because that bow was a treasure – made by Voirin and belonged to Ysaye.

Today that bow would be worth well over $100,000, but once it's damaged a bow immediately loses half its value even though a repair can be perfect and the bow even stronger than before. If it's a clean break, for example, they put in two pins which they cross and glue. But Stern's reaction was terrible anger and distress. Leading the second violin was a bloke called Bill Glass, a real Aussie. 'Serve the bugger right!', he muttered. Stern broke his journey back to America to go to Vatelot, the great bow master in Paris, to fix it.

Another vivid image in my mind from my time with the MSO was hearing the young David Helfgott – I think he was sixteen – playing in the ABC Instrumental and Vocal Competition. I thought he had extraordinary talent, that nobody could play like him.[25] In fact, the prize went to Roger Woodward who was a few years older, but I felt that Helfgott should have won. A couple of years later, Helfgott got a scholarship to the Royal College in London and studied under the great Cyril Smith, who apparently said that he was in the same league as Horowitz.

What's happened to Helfgott since is a tragedy, though there is something childlike and appealing about him now but his playing is strange. His illness has cost him. I've actually seen him get up during a concert and go to ask his wife what he's meant to be playing. It's sad, because he was a genuinely outstanding young musician.

After three years in Melbourne, I told Annette that if I was going to play in an orchestra for the rest of my life, it would have to be in England where there was so much variety. I simply didn't want to settle for the orchestra here. She accepted that and I decided to work up a Bartók piece in readiness for auditions. It was a hard piece, but I learned it and could play it well. And so we went back to England and the very day after we arrived I had a phone call from Louise, who was a fixer for the London orchestras. 'Chris! You're back', she cried. 'Can you come to Italy tomorrow on tour?' 'But we've only just got here', I protested. 'Meet us in Venice?' she said, and I did – no audition, nothing. That's what London could be like for a musician.

> Annette: Chris was so thrilled with Australia when we first went. He thought it was wonderful, and when we went back to England you would have thought that he was an ambassador for Australia, but nobody was interested, absolutely nobody.

The phone never stopped ringing. You'd be asked 'Can you do so and so, and so and so?', and you'd say, 'Yes, OK'. It was as simple as that. You just got out your diary and worked out the dates. I was a freelance viola player and was never short of work, never. It was wonderful. Among others, I played with the English Chamber Orchestra, the London Mozart Orchestra, the Royal Philharmonic, the Philomusica, the London String Quartet and the Oromonte Trio – all marvellous ensembles.

The Oromonte Trio

The name 'Oromonte' means 'mountain of gold' and came from the second violinist, who had studied with Szymon Goldberg. It was a tribute to him – 'berg' being German for mountain. The leader of the Oromonte, Perry Hart, was Australian, from Sydney. She was a lovely person. The cellist, Bruno Schreker, was half-Czech and used to say he was Heinz 57. When we were invited to play in Italy, they told us that we had to change our name to 'Monteoro', as Oromonte made no sense in Italian. It would be like calling Monteverdi 'Verdimonte'. To the annoyance of the Italian organisers, we refused to change.

One year, the Oromonte Trio was invited to play at the prestigious York Music Festival. Our concert was broadcast live and we played with a great American flautist, Elaine Shaffer. She was a gorgeous woman, married to Efrem Kurtz, a famous Russian conductor, an awfully funny man but full of himself. He was a pain during rehearsals. He kept interrupting, telling us to sit one way for the Mozart and another way for the Beethoven.

We were playing five or six pieces in the concert, picking up our music and our chairs and moving in between. The major work was an extremely complex, difficult work by Schoenberg, written when the composer was ill in hospital. Unlike the other two in the trio, I had never played it before. It's a great piece and was going well so I was hugely relieved when it was nearly over. I turned the last page only to discover the other side wasn't there. I freaked. My God, what to do? You can't fake a piece like that. I turned to Bruno and said, 'I ain't got a last page'. His bow went wooooooo! Perry was a nervous wreck anyway and nearly dropped her bow. There were two bars left before my music ran out.

It was a big event and the hall was packed. I thought, I'll just have to make light of it. What else can I do? I got to the bottom of my page, stopped and said, 'Sorry – I haven't got the last page!' There was dead silence. It was horrible, horrible. We searched our stands, music was flying everywhere. Then Bruno found it. What had happened was that we had changed places so much, picking up our music as we went, that I had left it behind. That piece was not a normal trio with three movements. It only had one movement and was all connected, so you couldn't pick up from anywhere. We just went back a yard and started again. This was really, really the worst experience of my musical life.

The next day we got *The Times*, *The Observer* and all the big London papers and *The Yorkshire Post*. All the reviews of the concert were good and I thought, thank God for that! Later on that year, however, when we were playing at the Edinburgh Festival, I was staying with a mathematician friend who said, 'I suppose you were the idiot in York who lost your last page'. I was surprised that he knew about it. 'Didn't you read *The Manchester Guardian*?' he asked. 'No', I told him, 'it was the only paper we couldn't find next morning'. Everybody hated Gerald Gardner, *The Guardian*'s famous music critic, because if he could find anything bad to say, he would say it. Apparently he wrote, 'It's a pity the continuity of the work was impaired by one of the players having mislaid his last page'. 'I knew it would be you', my friend laughed.

Dennis East

There was a violinist in London called Dennis East, who, before the war, was one of England's most brilliant up-and-coming young violin soloists. Annette and I met him when he was teaching at the London College of Music. He used to give concerts in schools around the country and invited us to join him. It was quite well paid, was an entertaining day out, and we became very close to Dennis.

He had been called up at eighteen, sent to South East Asia and ended up in the Japanese prisoner of war camp at Changi. Australians tend to think that they were the only ones there, but thousands of Englishmen were also incarcerated in Changi. Men from all sorts of backgrounds were there and Dennis said that it was amazing what they were able to make despite living in such horrible conditions.

One of the interpreters at Changi had been to Oxford or Cambridge and was sympathetic to the prisoners. He did what he could to enable them to have concerts and even found Dennis a violin. It was after one of the concerts that the Japanese asked for volunteers to work on the Thai–Burma Railway. Conditions would be wonderful, they told the prisoners, much better than at Changi. They would be cared for and their suffering over, as the prisoners had to be kept well enough to work. Dennis was one who volunteered and it turned out to be horrific. Thousands died.

When Dennis eventually got back to Changi, he was sick with cholera, typhoid and beriberi. There was nothing of him. He lay down on an old mattress and told his mates to leave him alone, that he wanted to die. Someone came up to him and told him that he wasn't going to die, that he would look after him. This man turned out to be an Australian doctor – one of several who did incredible work at Changi. His name was Lloyd Cahill.

A few years ago the ABC did a series on the Thai–Burma Railway on Sunday afternoons. One day they mentioned a Dr Cahill and I thought, that must be him! I wrote care of the ABC and got this letter back, dated 5 July 1984, sent from Pinball in New South Wales.

> Dear Mr Martin
>
> I wish to thank you for your gracious letter which eventually found me only two days ago. I well remember your great friend Dennis East and I'm delighted to hear that all is well with him. I had heard a few details about his career and his success. Nothing gives me more pleasure. And to learn that what little help I was able to offer him has had such an outstanding reward.
>
> I hope to visit England again early in 1985. Maybe on this occasion I will have the courage to catch up and seek him out.
>
> Thank you again for your wonderful letter which I will always treasure.
>
> Yours sincerely
> Lloyd Cahill

Next time I saw Dennis, I told him that I had written to Lloyd and he said, 'I know. I saw him when he came to England. We had lunch together.'

I have a book on my shelves called *The Naked Island,* by Russell Braddon – an Australian.[26] It's a really unforgiving book because Braddon suffered horribly at the hands of the Japanese. This is an extract in which he mentions Dennis:

> The Concert Party also flourished because it commanded the enthusiastic support of a young Japanese interpreter called Terai Terai, a peace-time professor of English in a Nipponese university, who was deemed by almost everyone to be pro-British. He was young, slim, had a pleasant face and was

always glad to find in Singapore such improbable commodities as strings for a violin or women's gowns, or makeup materials or whatever it was that the performers needed. All he asked in return was a little conversation – preferably not about the war, which he hated.

Meanwhile, Changi's irrepressible energy, the energy of ten thousand Britons cooped up without any contact with the outside world – burst out in a thousand different directions. There were courses on every subject and every language: there were societies to discuss every hobby and every sport: and there were little theatres playing everything from Shakespeare to 'Journey's End': there were concerts of classical music and concert parties which weren't classical at all. On my first night back in Changi I could have gone to any one of four plays or two musical shows: I could have heard Dennis East – peace-time violinist under Sir Thomas Beecham – give a recital.

When I was a boy, the BBC had a programme called Voices of Our Violin where a well-known violinist played for quarter of an hour. I used to listen. One day soon after the war ended, the violinist was Dennis East. The programme was live and Dennis was terrible. I thought, 'That guy can't play. What's going on?' When we met, I told him I had heard his broadcast. 'I couldn't do another one', he said. 'My nerves are shattered.'

Dennis married twice and had a daughter, Angela, who studied cello at the Royal Academy. When she was a student, she asked Dennis if she could bring her quartet home to play for him. There were four girls including Angela, and the second violin was Japanese; very young, born after the war, of course, but Japanese. At the sound of her voice, Dennis broke into a terrible sweat and left the room to get a glass of water. Angela followed him into the kitchen and asked him what was wrong. 'Your friend is delightful', he told her, 'but whenever she speaks, I feel ill. Go on with your rehearsal but I can't come back. Tell them I'm not well.'

I loved Dennis, he was a wonderful person and a wonderful player, but after the war he just didn't have the kind of energy and courage you need to get up and perform solo. The war cost him his musical career.

Simon and Naomi

Naomi had just been born when we met Dennis East, and Simon was just eighteen months old. We had to leave them with someone during the day when we went off with Dennis to play in the school concerts, and we found a wonderful person. Simon had been born at a teaching hospital in Enfield. Annette's placenta had packed up, so they decided to induce the baby. That evening, I was playing quartets in our tiny little flat. One of the violinists was an Israeli friend of Annette's called Avigdor and the other was Iona Brown, who led the Academy of St Martin-in-the-Fields for years and was a well-known solo performer. She was also a great friend of Annette's. I can't recall who was playing cello but I do remember the incredible thunderstorm that exploded around us as we played Beethoven. The wind howled and lightning crackled as we made music and Simon was born.

Strangely enough, Naomi, too, was born during a storm. I was playing with the London String Quartet somewhere in Norfolk and we were just about to launch into Debussy in the second half when someone came up to us and asked, 'Is one of you Mr Martin?' 'That's me!', I said. 'The hospital has phoned to say you have a baby girl.' They made an announcement to the audience and everyone was thrilled. After the concert, I got in the car to drive to Enfield, to the same hospital, and the rain was so heavy that I could hardly see. It was a fantastic storm. It was very late by the time I arrived but they let me in.

The life of a freelance musician can be physically exhausting. I used to do what they called 'sessions', which were held somewhere in south London, miles and miles from where we lived. They started at 10 a.m. I remember looking out of the window early on winter mornings, snow everywhere, and asking myself, how the hell am I going to get there in time? The car would be covered in snow and often wouldn't start, then the trains were late and I would have to allow at least two hours to get there. Players came from every direction and I was impressed that everyone always turned up despite the weather.

I nearly blotted my copybook horribly in London and it wasn't my fault. I had trouble with gallstones and when I had attacks, I writhed around on the floor in agony. Eventually the doctor said that I would have to have my gallbladder out and booked me in for Tuesday the following week. I was meant to be touring Wales with the English Chamber Orchestra, one of the most prestigious English orchestras, and rang the guy who ran it to say that I couldn't go. I think his name was Malcolm. I told him about my gallbladder operation and said I didn't want to risk playing in any concerts in case the pain struck and I collapsed. He said not to worry, as he would find someone else.

It so happens that the evening before my operation, I went to a concert and there was Malcolm. He looked at me coldly and said, 'What are you doing here? I thought you were in hospital.' 'I'm going tomorrow', I said, wondering whether he believed me. Being a fixer is a really hard job and I knew I was high on people's lists but I didn't want to get a reputation for letting people down. I did go to hospital the next day and was there a week. I also got lots more work with the English Chamber Orchestra, which I loved. My old teacher Cecil Aronowitz used to lead the violas and I sat next to him, which was lovely.

As well as sessions, I did a lot of travelling while Annette stayed at home looking after the children. We lived close to a park with a children's playground. Simon particularly loved the slide, even though it was quite high. He was fearless. I was once watching him and Naomi playing and it struck me that life would be so much better for them in Australia. The weather in England was so unreliable, and the schools were expensive. I wondered if we were making the right choice to stay in England for my work.

A number of things happened around that time; I wasn't well and had my gall bladder out, Annette's father died, and I was sounded out about the possibility of a job at the Conservatorium of Music at the University of Melbourne. Jack Glickman, the man who had the position, wanted to go to England but it was all up in the air. He wasn't sure when or if he was going.

In the meantime, we made up our minds and went back to Melbourne and I played with the MSO again. The ABC put huge pressure on me to sign a five-year contract, but I was reluctant because the University job was in the offing. While I was away with the orchestra on a tour of America, someone from the ABC again presented me with a contract. They said that they would understand if I had to break the contract, but I didn't trust them. It was just as well, because the University job did come my way and had I signed with the MSO for five years, I don't know how easy it would have been to get out of it.

Remembering Jacqueline du Pré

The distinguished English Chamber Orchestra (ECO) was unusual in that it had no full-time musicians. For each season, it employed people on a contract basis. Similarly in my day it didn't have a principal conductor, but there was a series of guest conductors including Raymond

Leopard, Sir Colin Davis and Daniel Barenboim.

We once did a tour in Sweden with Daniel Barenboim conducting. I always loved playing with the ECO, but I didn't get on well with Barenboim at all, though he is an amazing pianist and an excellent conductor. He's quite brilliant. Jacqueline du Pré was with us and in the early stages of her illness.[27] People were aware of it, as she didn't play at all. Normally she would have been the soloist. She was still vivacious and lovely and Barenboim was very attentive to her.

An odd thing happened on that tour. We were rehearsing *Verklärte Nacht* by Schoenberg, a marvellous piece with a great D major chord in the middle, like the entrance of a king. As we played it, the curtain shot back and there was Jackie standing like a queen. Everybody gasped. I don't think she knew the work well enough to plan that. She was looking through the gap listening to us when the curtain swung back by chance. I've had a few extraordinary sensations in my life and that was one of them.

Jackie was an outstanding musician. What happened to her was a tragedy. Many people feel that she did more to raise awareness of multiple sclerosis than she did for music. She used every means available to promote the cause for a cure and raised millions, making many public appearances and teaching. Her students adored her. She was only forty-two when she died – a very courageous, very positive woman.

I had an extraordinary encounter with Jackie's sister Hilary through one of my past students of the violin and one of my greatest friends, Elizabeth Wallfisch. Now one of the most famous baroque players in the world, she lives in London with her husband, Raphael Wallfisch, famous in his own right as a cellist. Libby and I love each other dearly and I often stayed with her and her family. I knew Raphael's parents many years before he and Libby met. His father Peter, a concert pianist, escaped Hitler's Germany, embarked on an international career and eventually settled in London. He played with a number of orchestras including the Mozart Players, which is where I met him.

Peter's wife Anita Lasker was a cellist and this saved her from the gas chamber in Auschwitz. When she arrived there, she was picked out by Alma Rosé who ran the female orchestra. Evidently Rosé grabbed as many musicians as she could and saved their lives by putting these women in the orchestra. Anita was the youngest and one of only two serious musicians in the orchestra.

Rosé was tough because she needed to be. She knew that if the orchestra didn't reach a certain standard, the players would be disposed of. She herself was a violinist and famous in Vienna as the founder of an orchestra called the Waltzing Girls of Vienna.[28] Her father, Arnold Rosé, had been leader of the Vienna Philharmonic Orchestra and her mother, Justine, was Gustav Mahler's sister. Arnold went to work one day soon after the Germans annexed Austria and they told him, 'You're gone'. It was as quick as that. Justine had died some years before but he and Alma escaped to London. Unfortunately Alma was invited to start an orchestra in Holland just before the Germans moved in. She was arrested there and sent to Auschwitz.

Anita talks about being sent for by Josef Mengele and going in terror of what to expect, only to be asked to play for him. He was a monster but he adored music. They all did. Anita survived the war and afterwards went to London where she became a founding member of the English Chamber Orchestra and met and married Peter Wallfisch. She later wrote an account of her experiences.[29]

A few years ago I was staying with the Wallfisches when Raphael suggested that I go with him to a village in the country, near Newbury, where he was giving a Sunday concert. His pianist picked us up and, as we drove, Raphael explained that we were going to the home of Jacqueline du Pré's sister Hilary and her husband Christopher Finzi. 'Kiffer', as everybody called him, was the son of the composer Gerald Finzi. Finzi famously had an affair with Jackie when she was staying with them in this house. Hilary wrote about it openly in her book.[30]

The concert was a private affair in a small church, followed by a grand reception at the Finzi's house. I didn't take to Kiffer at all, but Hilary I liked enormously. She was charming and down-to-earth. She came up to me and said, 'I believe you knew Jackie?' I talked about meeting Jackie at a ten-day summer school in Dartington and said that I took a photograph there of her, along with Joan Dickson, Paul Tortelier and my wife Annette, all standing with their cellos. Like Annette, Jackie had studied with Tortelier in Paris, but he wasn't right for her. She later went to Russia and studied with Rostropovich, with whom she got on much better.

Hilary seemed thrilled to talk about Jackie and obviously adored her. She was warm and utterly unpretentious, whereas her husband was a party type. When you spoke to him, you had the impression that he was looking for someone else more important to move on to. It was an interesting afternoon.

And Yehudi Menuhin

Two or three of my greatest friends were in Yehudi Menuhin's Bath Festival Orchestra but I never played in it myself. I did play with Menuhin in one memorable concert with the London Mozart Players, at a castle near Munich called Schloss Elmau. Apparently it had been occupied by the Nazis during the war. Our conductor was Antal Dorati and we were going to be there over a long weekend. Everything was covered with snow and it was quite magical. The woman who owned the castle was charming.

Yehudi arrived with Diana Gould, his second wife. She was a ballet dancer and actress and took over his life. He adored her beyond anything you can imagine, absolutely adored her. He was a gentle, soft man and she was always there. When he came out to play, she came with him, gave him a little kiss, said, 'Good luck, darling!' and then sat down in the front row. We found it fascinating.

Quite a few people I knew went to the Yehudi Menuhin School in Cobham. I visited the school when I was teaching at Melbourne University. They didn't take many students – perhaps thirty or forty. Yehudi went around the world picking the best pupils and offering them scholarships. Nigel Kennedy went there and so did a friend of mine, Caroline Henbest, a very fine violin and viola player. You didn't get in to the Menuhin School unless you were outstanding.

I had an argument with the head man there. He wasn't a musician but an educator. I told him that he had a wonderful school with some incredible players, but they weren't all Nigel Kennedys. Some would go into orchestras. He said absolutely not, his students wouldn't play in orchestras. I pointed out to him that two days previously I had sat next to one of his past pupils in the English Chamber Orchestra. 'Ah', he said, 'chamber orchestras are an elite group'. He had meant that they wouldn't play in symphony orchestras. I said I didn't think that Mr Menuhin would agree with him, that as long as they had a good position in a great orchestra he would be happy. He didn't like that.

I love Nigel Kennedy. His playing is glorious though he committed the cardinal sin of making a recording of Vivaldi's *Four Seasons* and chatting in between. A lot of musicians I know hated that, but none of the hundreds of recordings of the *Four Seasons* has sold like Nigel's. He's made a lot of money and is over the top – he supports a football team!

The orchestra here loves him because he stays up half the night and plays jazz with them then turns up an hour late for rehearsals.

I was very close to Nigel's father, the cellist John Kennedy.[31] We worked together at Melbourne University for years but first met in London in the late 1950s, when we both played quartets with Manny Hurwitz one evening.[32] It was a relaxed gathering with friends and John played brilliantly. I knew of him because he was principal cellist with the Royal Philharmonic under Sir Thomas Beecham. His marriage was breaking up at the time we met and he left soon after for Australia. His wife was pregnant with Nigel, who grew up to become such a superb violinist that he has sold more classical CDs than any other artist ever.

There are so many wonderful young players around today, and people say that the standard is so much higher than it was fifty years ago. It's true that many, many more can play brilliantly but the standard is not higher, not artistically. There's nobody who plays like Michelangeli, or Horowitz, or Rubinstein. My son Ben agrees with me. We watched a DVD of Michelangeli together and it's incredible piano playing. I don't think you get the same artistry with today's youngsters, though technically they are fantastic. I heard a Sibelius concerto played by Sarah Chang when she was about twelve. It was more perfect than a live performance by Heifetz, but I wouldn't cross the road to hear it because it just didn't seize me by the throat, whereas I would run a hundred miles to hear Heifetz.

A chorus of conductors

When you go to a concert where there is a rapport between the orchestra and conductor, you can tell. It helps if the conductor really wants to make good music. One conductor I found hard to work with was George Solti. I was with the London Mozart Players when I worked with him and it wasn't a happy experience. The orchestra called him the 'screaming skull'. But he was right there with the music; he didn't miss much. André Previn, who conducted the London Symphony Orchestra when I played under him, was an absolute delight – very gentle, very nice and also very famous as he was married to Mia Farrow at the time. He got the result he wanted with an orchestra without being difficult or coercive, unlike Solti or another Hungarian, György Széll, who was extremely professional but hard on musicians. He didn't allow anything not to work.

One of the greatest conductors of my time was yet another Hungarian, Fritz Reiner, who became music director of the Chicago Symphony Orchestra in the early 1950s. He was a man with a bullet head, no neck, who looked like a bull. People were terrified of him. He was from the old school of conductors. You didn't argue with him, and he frightened you to death but he got extraordinary results. Recordings of his, especially Bartók, have never been bettered. He always conducted from memory with the tiniest beat, his eyes everywhere. There is a story about him conducting Beethoven's Seventh Symphony, which starts *dee da dee*. He glowered at the orchestra, muttered, 'There will be sackings', and growled in time to the beat, 'Many will have to go, yes many will have to go'. This went on for the whole introduction – about five minutes – and then the rhythm picked up, *bom bom bom,* and Reiner called out gleefully, ''Appy, 'appy, 'appy!'

He had a long baton but it hardly moved at the end, and one brass player complained that he couldn't see the beat. 'You'll see it tonight at the concert', barked Reiner. And so the concert came and the movement of the baton was so slight that the brass player put down his instrument and picked up a telescope. Apparently Reiner held up a small piece of paper on which he'd written: 'You're fired!'

One of the most memorable concerts I have ever played in was with Leonard Bernstein conducting the London Bach Orchestra. He didn't normally conduct small orchestras like that; he was a big orchestra man. One of the pieces we played was the Bach Magnificat. Bernstein obviously loved it. Everybody conducted Bach in more or less the same way in those days, with a choirmaster running the show rather than an orchestra conductor. The London Bach Orchestra had Dr Reginald Jakes – a lovely man but he didn't understand orchestras much. He relied on having good players and concentrated on the choir. With Bernstein, it was different. The way he rehearsed lifted the standard of the orchestra up and up. It was an amazing experience. I remember at the time wondering what was going on and how he was making it happen.

The second half of the programme was *Les Noces* by Stravinsky, an astonishing work – very hard to conduct. There are no strings, only percussion, solo voices, a boys' choir and four pianos. Martha Argerich and her husband Stephen Kovacevich played two of the pianos. I don't remember the other pianists. It's a very complex piece and at one point

Martha seemed to be floundering. Like a shot, Bernstein was with her and she was right, though you wouldn't have picked it unless you knew the music. Bernstein was conducting from memory, of course. He loved that music so much and wanted us to love it too.

I often think about Bernstein and what it was about his conducting that was different. Other conductors lifted standards in different ways. Solti conducting *Adoremus*, for example, was always brilliant because he raised the whole thing with his personality, but conducting smaller groups and smaller works was not his thing and you felt that he was irritated by them. He wanted things played a certain way and if the orchestra wasn't used to that, it didn't work. With Bernstein, you could tell from the first note that he was in love with the music and the orchestra responded to the emotion of it. A good friend of mine, Tess, was once playing a solo in one of his concerts and he asked her to replay it during rehearsals just so that we could all hear it again. He was as excited as a child.

Otto Klemperer was a strange man but the Philharmonia in London liked him. He became its principal conductor in 1959. His secretary was a man called Mendelssohn. The two of them were walking along Oxford Street one day and when they reached the huge HMV shop there, Klemperer insisted on going in. Some members of the orchestra happened to be in the record section and heard Klemperer asking what Beethoven recordings they had. The assistant mentioned von Karajan and a number of other big conductors. 'Have you got Klemperer?' he was asked. 'No sir, we don't. Why do you particularly want Klemperer?' 'Because I am Klemperer.' 'Ha!', said the assistant, pointing to Klemperer's companion, 'and I suppose he's Beethoven?' 'No', said Klemperer, 'he's Mendelssohn!'

The worst conductor I've ever worked with was a Dane called Nils Gruen. I was the lead viola in the Philomusica in London, a small orchestra, and the leader was a great friend, Carl Pini, who is now in Sydney. Gruen was then in his fifties, I think, and in a relationship with an extremely rich Scottish woman who financed him. They lived in her gorgeous apartment in London. He heard that the Philomusica was seriously in debt and decided to buy it. He said that he would pay off the orchestra's debt if he could conduct it, and the board agreed. He was appalling.

One day at the end of a practice, he told me that he wanted the orchestra to have really good instruments and he was going to start the ball rolling by lending me his viola. I was shocked. It was a Gaspar, which he had bought from Hills in London and it had belonged to Paganini. An incredible instrument and big – about 16½ inches – bigger than mine. I used it for rehearsals that day and for a concert that night and then took it back to Nils. He tried to persuade me to keep playing it, but I said no, one day he would want it back and it would kill me. It was a beautiful instrument and would probably be worth more than £1 million today.

One of the concerts was particularly embarrassing because Sir Adrian Boult was in the audience. Carl Pini led that concert. He would turn to the orchestra and gesture and they followed him. Nils hated it because Carl was taking over in front of him. At the interval, Nils went up to Carl and said, 'Would you mind letting me conduct the second half?' 'If you conducted properly, I'd let you do it but you don't', said Carl. The second half was just as bad as the first. Carl and I both wrote letters of resignation after that concert.

After we left, Nils recorded all the Brandenburg concertos, hiring Frederick Riddle as lead viola.[33] Frederick was the finest viola player in England. He led for Sir Thomas Beecham and all the great orchestras. Nils lent him the Gaspar for the recording. I later heard that Nils and the Scottish lady split up and he lost access to all that money. He might have had to give the viola back, I don't know. Just as well I didn't take it.

I never played with Sir Thomas Beecham but Carl Pini told me a delightful story about him. Carl's father, Anthony Pini, was principal cellist with the Royal Philharmonic Orchestra and Beecham asked him one day how Carl was going with the violin. He's doing alright, Carl's father said, but needs a decent violin and I can't afford it. He explained that he had his eye on a Bergonzi at Hills but they were asking £4,500 and he was £2,000 short. After rehearsal that day, Beecham gave Anthony a cheque for the Bergonzi and said that he could repay him little by little through his wages. No hurry. So Carl got his Bergonzi and had it for years and years. He loved it.

Carl Pini was originally called Anthony after his father, who also played the violin professionally. When Carl became an important violinist, it was decided that he should use his second name, Carl, to avoid confusion. The strange thing is that his father was always known as Charlie.

In the 1970s, Carl was concertmaster to the Philharmonia in London and invited me to a concert in which Itzhak Perlman was performing. Perlman had polio when he was four, so comes onto the stage on crutches and plays sitting down. The concert was filmed, and watching afterwards you saw the camera pause on Carl's face and it had this look of pure joy and delight at such artistry. It is great to see such admiration from one musician to another, and Carl's no slouch himself! He had invited me backstage during the interval and I found him with Perlman, in his dressing room sitting in a wheelchair. As he introduced us, the door opened and in came Jacqueline du Pré in her wheelchair pushed by Daniel Barenboim. We all hugged each other. It was so poignant to see the two wheelchairs together.

You can count on the fingers of one hand the women who have made it to the top. Simone Young is one, Marin Alsop another. It's a miracle for any woman to make it because of the antagonism they face. In Vienna, for example, you don't stand a chance if you're a woman. They don't want to know. A friend of mine who plays in the Vienna Philharmonic was saying recently that if a man and a woman went for a job and the woman was slightly better, they would still take the man. It will take a long time for that to change there, just as it did in England, although the BBC always had women in the orchestra and small orchestras did, too, but the symphony orchestras held out for years.

Herbert von Karajan once did the unforgivable with the Berlin Philharmonic. The whole orchestra sits in on auditions and has a say in the outcome. There would be no question of accepting a woman but when the clarinet player Sabina Myer auditioned, von Karajan overrode the orchestra. He was powerful enough to say, 'She's my clarinet', and that was it. She's a fantastic musician, famous now, and played with the Berlin Philharmonic for years.

James Gallway also auditioned for the Berlin Philharmonic and it was such a gruelling process that he told them he didn't want the job. He went in the end, of course; they really wanted him. He is a great player and I knew him well in London. We played together occasionally in the London Mozart Players. Jimmy was always very bolshy, very funny. If a conductor was running late, he'd say, 'I'm going home. I'm not hanging around here. Come on, let's go!' The thing is, if you're that good, you can move from here to there and everybody wants you and you can behave – not quite but almost – as you want.

The London Mozart Players were founded by Harry Blech.[34] It was a very good orchestra of about thirty performers and I loved playing with it. Harry conducted it for years, and sometimes when we were engaged to do concerts we had a guest conductor, which orchestras mostly enjoy – though Solti was a challenge.

Harry was a lovely man – a fine violinist and very good musician, but a poor conductor. He always had trouble with the beat in the Schumann piano concerto, for example, because it goes against the music. He found a wonderful solution because he was a very musical man. He just kept the beat simple and kept out of the orchestra's way. It worked perfectly, as the orchestra didn't really need him. Another problem he had was missing the end of cadenzas. Jacqueline du Pré once did this run-up at the end of the first movement of the Schumann cello concerto and Harry became terribly confused. At the end of it, she gave him the loveliest smile.

The London Mozart Players did a lot of travelling around England and we were once rehearsing for a concert in a church hall when the leader, Robert Masters, almost lost his Stradivarius violin. We were taking a break and Nannie Jamieson, another violinist, walked down the aisle and through the heavy old church doors. She didn't realise that Robert was behind her. I remember at the time thinking that he was silly to hold his violin in front of him. Anyway the doors swung back, hitting the bridge of Robert's Strad. He was furious with Nanny and in a terrible state, but when he put the bridge back up he realised that there wasn't a mark on his violin.

When we came to Australia, one of the best known conductors here was Henry Krips, resident conductor of the South Australian Symphony Orchestra, who emigrated from Vienna before the war.[35] I never played with him, though Annette and I both played in Europe with his half-brother, Josef Krips, an exceptionally fine conductor. Some of his recordings of Beethoven and Mozart are said to be the best ever. Henry was famous in Australia for being the first to conduct Mahler here. I heard that at the first Mahler concert, the crowd went wild and Henry held up the score to the audience and said, 'Don't clap me, clap Mahler'.

I have a friend who was a freelance horn player and he was booked to go and play with the South Australian Symphony Orchestra. For some reason, this fellow shaved from top to toe and was as bald as a baby. After a number of rehearsals, the night of the concert came and

Henry Krips walked to the podium to begin. He looked around the orchestra and spotted this strange horn player with a thick head of hair. 'Who is this?', cried Krips. Turning to the audience, he said, 'He has never rehearsed with me. I don't do this concert.' He stormed off followed by the leader, who said, 'Mr Krips, it's the same man. It's just that he's wearing a wig.' Finally convinced, he returned to the podium, apologised and raised his baton.

Henry Krips was one of several high-profile conductors who came to Australia either just before or just after the war. We had Georges Tzipine in Melbourne. They were very good but they weren't top rank conductors. There was no way the top conductors would have stayed in Australia, as they had such big careers in Europe. We did, however, get top people visiting, often staying two or three months and conducting orchestras in different states.

When Malcolm Sargent came to Melbourne, he always stayed at Government House. He was very much 'Sir Malcolm', very aristocratic. The orchestras didn't like him but I think he was a good conductor and a good man. There was great rivalry between him and Sir Thomas Beecham. For years, Sargent was Dr Malcolm Sargent – he was a Doctor of Music. When he got his knighthood, someone in the orchestra said to Beecham, 'Sir Thomas, I believe Sir Malcolm has been knighted', and Beecham said, 'Really? I knew he'd been doctored.' Another time, Sargent went to the Middle East and his convoy was fired on by Arabs. Beecham's response on being told this was, 'Are the Arabs so musical?' Sargent died of cancer and was very courageous in facing his illness. The Australian Doctors' Orchestra has raised money for the Sir Malcolm Sargent Cancer Fund for Children in Victoria.

One great exception about top-ranking conductors not coming here as residents in the years after the war is Eugene Goossens. He was a marvellous, marvellous conductor – in a class of his own – and had recorded with all kinds of famous people in Europe, including Jascha Heifetz. He conducted the Sydney Symphony Orchestra for nine years but he fled in disgrace back to Europe in 1956, a year after he was knighted by the Queen. There was a real witch-hunt and some think that he was set up, though that's unlikely. Australia in the 1950s was incredibly narrow-minded and parochial. What happened to Goossens was a tragedy.[36]

Something similar but less serious happened to my friend Jan Sedivka in Queensland. He emigrated to Queensland in the early 1960s, to teach violin at the Conservatorium. He was a very successful man in every way, but there were people who didn't like him and took exception to his lifestyle and his late night parties. He was hounded and even subjected to police surveillance and planned to go back to London in disgust, but somebody enticed him to Tasmania where he established the finest string school that Australia has ever known.[37] I went many times to his brilliant Summer School and was put up at the university and given a car, which was nice. I met Hartmut Lindemann there and he became one of my dearest friends.

One of the most popular and successful of the overseas conductors who have settled in Australia is Hiroyuki Iwaki. He came as guest conductor in 1973 and then became chief conductor to the MSO in 1974 and has stayed twenty-three years. The orchestra liked him very much and he was appointed Conductor Laureate in 1990. He was a nice man and a fine conductor.

Markus Stenz, who came after Iwaki, was one of the nicest blokes you could meet.[38] When he arrived, he said that he was going to do all the Mahler symphonies – and he did. To some extent the MSO felt like guinea-pigs, but a big orchestra in Europe would have gone to a major conductor for Mahler, so it gave Stenz the opportunity to build up his repertoire here and we did get the first performances. Ashkenazy, on the other hand, is a much older man and he went to Sydney with an extensive repertoire which he knows well. He's a fine musician but not such a strong conductor, however the orchestra likes him so much that it's OK.

It amazes me that conductors today seem to be able to conduct anything. Some things would frighten the life out of me – pieces I feel that I couldn't do justice to. I never wanted to take them on.

Music camps and summer schools

Most quartets run music camps or summer schools. It's hard but rewarding, the people are generally delightful and the camaraderie is fantastic. I was involved with a lot of music camps, particularly when I played with the Edinburgh Quartet and later with the London Quartet. They are very popular and mostly for anybody who wants to go, which can be difficult if they can't play at orchestral level. Sorting people into groups would take all day, with some only wanting to be with this or that person or to play a particular kind of music. At the end, you were always left with people you didn't know what to do with. They couldn't play well and were only there for the social activities. We called this group 'the sink' and found something simple that they could manage to play together.

At one music camp that I was at in England, there was an exceptionally weak quartet. The leader was an anxious, middle-aged lady who was a terrible player but loved playing. The second violin was a boy of fifteen, a nervous kind of boy, and the viola player was an elderly lady who was even more anxious than the leader. The cellist was a greengrocer from up north, called George. George had all the confidence whereas the others had none. We decided to give this group Haydn's Bird Quartet which starts off with the second violin and the viola playing '*yup up up up*' – just quavers. Then the first violin comes in, followed by the cello with *bom bom bom bom* – all arpeggios.

When it came to the concert, the viola got into such a panic that she infected the boy and they started going *blip blup blup blup*. It completely unnerved the first violin and her notes tumbled all the way down. George was waiting for his entry and you could see him thinking, 'What's going on here? I have to do something about this rubbish.' So he came in *BONG, BONG, BONG, BONG*! An enormous sound that crashed through the whole group. You couldn't believe what you were hearing. It was even worse with the repeat, as the leader's bow spluttered all the way down the violin and she couldn't play the notes. They were all completely undone by this stage and again George came in like an armoured tank. Tears were running down my cheeks because it was the funniest thing I've ever heard. They got to the end – the great C major chord – but all you heard was George. He flung his bow in the air in triumph, stood up and beamed at the audience. The others just couldn't move; they were paralysed. George yelled at them, 'Get oop! Get oop!' They scrambled to their feet, utterly demoralised.

George came up to me after and said, 'How was that, then?' 'Well George, you certainly enjoyed yourself.' 'I don't know what's going on with that lot', he replied. 'I don't know what they were doing. I had to save it.' So George was a hero. Funny little man, nice man. I think he was from Halifax – somewhere 'oop north'. I think the viola went into a nursing home soon after.

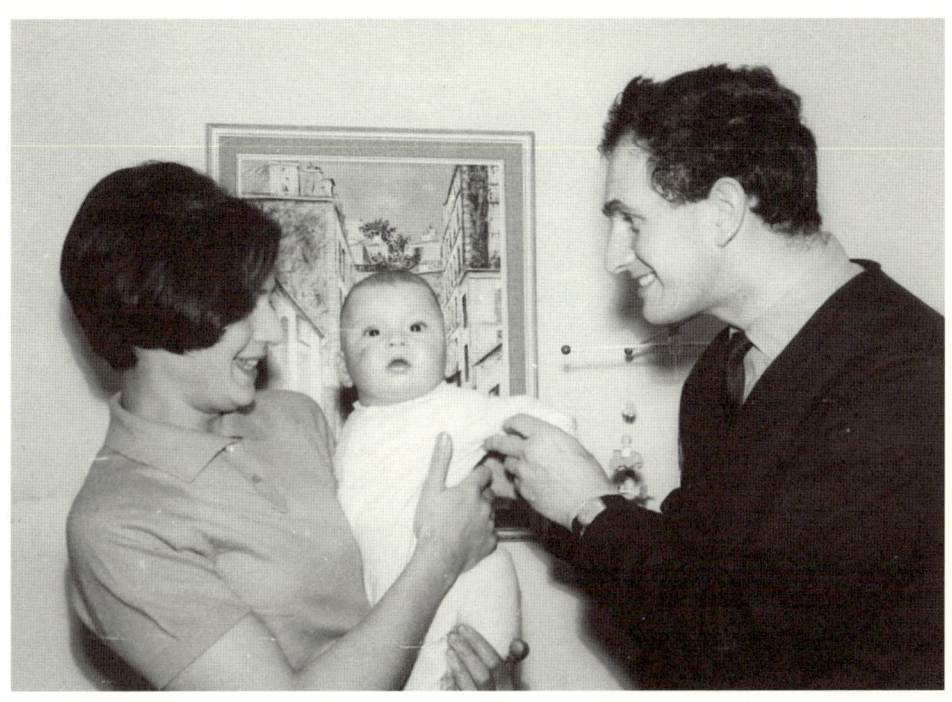

Annette and Chris with their son Simon, born in Enfield in 1965, when his parents were working as freelance musicians.

A photograph of Naomi and Simon taken when the family returned to Australia. Simon (right) is holding their pet guinea-pig, Michi, who was reluctant to learn the piano.

Above Four cellists at
the summer school in
Dartington Hall. From left
to right: Annette Martin,
Jacqueline du Pré, Paul
Tortelier and Joan Dickson.
Photo: Christopher Martin.

Left Anita Lasker,
cellist, in 1938.
Photo: courtesy of Margaret Clune.

Above & below
The London String Quartet with Carl Pini, Roy Gillard,
Chris Martin and Carl's father, cellist Anthony Pini.

Jan Sedivka and Chris Martin at the Jan Sedivka Summer School in Hobart.

Gillian, Chris and Annette at one of the National Music Camps held at
Geelong Grammar School in Corio. All three were involved in music camps,
all their professional lives.

Elizabeth Wallfisch (Hunt) with Christopher Martin. Theirs was a friendship forged through a shared passion for music and a capacity to entertain audiences.

Quartet practice at the Mount Buller Chamber Music Summer School,
with Annette Martin, cello (left), Osman Ozturk, violin, Miki Pohl, viola
and Rowan Thomas, violin.

Above The Australian Doctors'
Orchestra, founded by
Miki Pohl in 1992, playing
Beethoven's Triple Concerto
in C at its tenth anniversary
concert at the Sydney Town Hall
in 2002 with Elizabeth Wallfisch,
violin, Niall Brown, cello and
Benjamin Martin, piano.
Photo: courtesy of Miki Pohl.

Below Nicolette Fraillon rehearsing the Australian Doctors'
Orchestra in Sydney when Chris was ill with cancer.

P J KEATING

LEVEL 1
31 BLIGH STREET
SYDNEY AUSTRALIA

12 February 2001.

Dear Mr Martin,

Many thanks for your recent letter concerning Josif Hassid.

Of the eight or so things he recorded in 1940 the 'La Capricieuse' is the piece which most or best illustrates his prodigious skills; the pity is it appears that those pieces were all that was ever recorded.

Our times lack pieces in which a little music is implied, the items they must be short so a long or an encore piece is about

TEL: 61-2-9223 7282 FAX: 61-2-9223 7280 GPO BOX 2598 SYDNEY NSW 2001

On hearing that Paul Keating was something of an aficionado of classical recordings and admired Josef Hassid's rendition of Elgar's *La Capricieuse*, Chris Martin wrote to him saying that he too greatly respected the young Polish pianist who tragically all one can propose.

But little gems do pop up and not always historic meanings. Even so, Hassid is not likely to be easily eclipsed.

Those Germans, of whom you speak do take their music seriously having spoke much of it; it is when they have Grander ideas they give the rest of us a problem. I'm all for more German Concert halls.

Warmest regards to you

Paul Keating

developed schizophrenia and died in 1950 at the age of 27 after brain surgery. Chris was delighted to receive a hand-written response from Paul Keating which he kept, framed, on his wall. (Letter reproduced with permission from Paul Keating.)

On a visit to the Mount Buller chamber Music Summer School, Chris caught up with good friend Wilma Smith, concertmaster of the Melbourne Symphony Orchestra.

At the pinnacle of his career, Ron Davey conducting the Tiverton Youth Orchestra on 15 April 1977. Photo: *The Guardian*.

Chris with Ron Davey on one of his many return visits to Tiverton. He never forgot
that it was Ron who opened his mind and heart to music.

Chris's joy at seeing the Chamber Strings of Melbourne win the overall prize at the twenty-seventh International Youth and Music Festival in Vienna was somewhat marred when the crystalware arrived in Melbourne in a thousand pieces.

Above Chris Martin conducting the Chamber Strings of Melbourne in Paris, giving the last concert in their 2009 European tour.

Left Chris, ever the entertainer, busking in the streets of China for a lark during a Chamber Strings of Melbourne tour. This was one of Chris's favourite photos.

Photo: courtesy of the Chamber Strings of Melbourne.

Chris conducting the Australian Doctors' Orchestra in the Melba Hall, Melbourne.
Photo: courtesy of Miki Pohl.

Chris rehearsing the Bartók viola concerto with the Corpus Medicorum and solo viola, Hartmut Lindemann. Photo: courtesy of Corpus Medicorum.

Miki Pohl: You weren't in Buller last year (2009) when four little old ladies came quietly out on stage. The second violin wore a tiny blue cardigan and was a wizened eighty-three or eighty-four. The first violin was about seventy-eight, the cellist was the youngest in her mid sixties and the viola was in her late seventies. The spokesperson was the lady in the blue cardigan. Each group at Buller has to give itself a name and she said, 'We thought we'd call ourselves the Oh My God Quartet, as in "Oh my God, we have to play in front of you!" We want to play a piece by Shostakovich, the tenth quartet about war, and we'll just play the first movement.' As they sat down, they sort of metamorphosed and transformed, and just went for it. It was such a Susan Boyle moment. There was a universal intake of breath. It turned out they were all ex-pros from the Sydney Symphony Orchestra! It was a great moment; everyone went ballistic. Of course the little old lady playing second violin knew exactly how to set it up. They were such fun, the four of them.

What makes the Mount Buller Chamber Music Summer School in Victoria so special is that people can only go as a group, but even so, you still get some funny experiences. There was one group that was quite weak and I asked Joan Dickson, who was working with them, what they were going to play for the concert. 'The slow movement from Beethoven's Opus 135', she said. 'My God, Joan!' I said. 'That's one of the pinnacles of music.'

The last movement of this work is famous because Beethoven added words on top of some of the notes and no one knows what he meant. The earlier orchestral part has 'Must it be', and later the music loudly breaks *boom BA bum, bom BA bum*. And he's put, 'It MUST be, it MUST be'. If you want to be trivial about Beethoven – and some people are because they think that Beethoven couldn't be trivial himself – some think that the landlady had come in and said, 'I want my money!' And he said, 'Must it be?' But seriously, it's all conjecture.

Yet the slow movement – the one before this – is the most amazing piece. I couldn't believe that Joan would give it to this group, but they played it with such feeling – it was wonderful. Joan made them play long bows because if you change the bow a lot, it ruins it. And they weren't nervous. Their music had something simply because they were so committed. Their playing was lifted up by the music.

Miki Pohl: I think it's very generous the way professionals get involved with amateurs and give us their best. I once sat with Kim Bishop, Director of Suzuki Violin Teacher Training in Victoria and a good friend of yours. The particular group we were listening to always chose pieces beyond them, always played badly, but it didn't deter them. They could play something less challenging quite well but they felt they had to stretch themselves. I was struggling through a Shostakovich and my cellist, Cate Mooney, turned to me and said, 'I can't stand that they always play in the cracks, they never play the notes!' It's true. If you can't play that sort of music spot on, then it just doesn't work. Anyway we sat through this and I turned to Kim and asked, 'Why do you enjoy that?' She said, 'I enjoy the integrity of effort.'

Annette: Not much was happening in Australia in the 1950s and the National Music Camp was the most extraordinary experience for young musicians living here at that time.[41]

It happened because of the partnership between John Bishop and Ruth Alexander, particularly Ruth. She had this vision. It brought students together from different states. They slept in dormitories and got to know each other well. Each day had a structure: tutorials and orchestra in the morning, a rest after lunch and then chamber music in the afternoon. In the evening, the staff would play to the students. Those two weeks were so exciting that they would stay with you the whole year until the next time. The music camps at Geelong Grammar are particularly deep in my memory. There was a little path lined with lavender leading to the new music school there, which was all big glass windows and the smell of the cork floors. Music camp was on a much smaller scale then than now – much smaller. It was life-giving.

When Chris and I came back from England and became involved with music camps as tutors, the standard was higher as so many more kids were learning music. We would take different groups, he the violas and me the cellos but mostly he was conducting. We would also take part in chamber music concerts with other tutors. The structure was still much the same, but what used to be the first orchestra was now the third orchestra. The standard of the first orchestra was extraordinary. That in itself made a difference.

Today the National Music Camp has become very streamlined and they bring in people from overseas. In our day, you were paid a pittance; you did it because you could see the point, because you wanted to do it. There's something very special about kids struggling with something which is beyond them and finding whichever way they can to be able to do it. Everything has since become very polished. With all this equipment now and wonderful technique and everything they can do, I think you lose some of that excitement of what it means to not be able to do something but wanting to very much.

The University of Melbourne

In 1972, I took up the position of Head of Strings at the University of Melbourne. It meant teaching violin and viola, as well as some conducting, coaching in chamber music and conducting the faculty orchestra. It involved doing work that I had never done before, and conducting difficult pieces such as Prokofiev and Stravinsky that required knowledge and technique. I found that what I did was fine. I loved it and loved the association with young people. I generally got on well with all the staff, most of whom are now dead. We had enormous conversations. I was there for twenty-six years and worked with some outstanding young musicians. Elizabeth Wallfisch would probably be the most eminent among them and is the one who means more to me than any other soloist who has been a pupil.

I first met her when she was about fifteen or sixteen and still at school. Her teacher was my colleague Jack Glickman and when he went off to London for a sabbatical he asked me to take Libby on. Her father was a professor of Engineering and an amateur clarinettist. Her stepmother taught the cello. Both Libby and her twin sister Tanya played instruments – Libby, the violin and Tanya, the cello. They were tremendously talented.

I found Libby a joy to teach because she was so receptive. She was preparing for an ABC music competition and I suggested that she play Tchaikovsky, which she adored. Tchaikovsky works well for competitions because, if you play well, it's brilliant and tuneful. We worked hard at that and she liked the style that it was played in. I think she stood a good chance of winning. Unfortunately, Jack came back before the competition and wanted Libby to play a Mendelssohn piece that he had worked on with her. She played well but didn't win, which was disappointing.

Libby has gone on to a brilliant career, but quite apart from being an amazing musician she is the most infectious person on the stage I have ever known. I call it 'infectious' because she only has to walk out and the audience melts. Even if she didn't play at all, that connection would still be there.

Conducting the orchestra at the Conservatorium brought me into contact with students whom I would not necessarily have known just through strings. One particularly gifted musician was Genevieve Lacey. She played the oboe beautifully and I couldn't understand why she had this thing about the recorder. The oboe was her second instrument and she agreed to play it in the orchestra because I asked her. Then at one of our concerts she played several pieces on the recorder. Tears flowed as I listened and I thought, 'This girl is wonderful'. I can't remember what she played, just that it was incredibly moving. It was obvious that she had something very special and I said to her, 'You stick to your recorder'.

When I first went to the Conservatorium, the student orchestra was outstanding. Things changed after 1974 when the School of Music was established as part of the newly formed Victorian College of the Arts. John Hopkins was the inaugural Dean of the School of Music. What the College told young people was that if they just wanted to make music without doing all the academic work required by the University, they should go there. Students would come to me for advice and I would tell them that if they just wanted to be a performer, they would certainly be better going to the College of the Arts otherwise they would be immersed in their studies, as the University was becoming more and more academic. It always had the practice of Music, too, but students did not get as much time with their instruments there as they did at the College. The College turned out musicians, that's what it was for. Like the Australian Academy of Music, it did not award any degrees. I pointed out to students that if they wanted to teach, this was a big drawback.

We had a strange situation at one time with the College of the Arts. There was a director who informed the Music staff that she was going to change the payment system. 'If you have one pupil', she said, 'you are merely regurgitating the same lesson with the next'. We explained that you can't teach music any other way – you have individual lessons and you have class lessons, that's the way it has always been. Her response was that casual teachers would be paid for the first two hours of each day and not the remaining three or four hours.

There was a great outcry and several resignations, especially the MSO people who were teaching part-time. It's true that most subjects can be taught in classes which can be repeated, but not the teaching of an instrument. It involves carefully watching the student, each of whose needs will be different. This director's approach didn't last long but should never have happened in the first place.

Naturally there were students at the Conservatorium who were good but not outstanding. Many of them played in my chamber music group and still come up to me today and say how much they loved it. One of my good friends, Cathy Weiss, told me that she learned more from playing with the chamber music group than anything else. Cathy is a violinist and a close friend of Libby Wallfisch. She, too, plays mostly baroque music now and has done well in London. I think that if Libby had stayed with the classical violin repertoire, she wouldn't have done as well as she has, as the world is full of brilliant violinists. She is more musical than most but the competition is enormous. Once she branched out into baroque, Libby found her strengths. She adores the music that she plays and is sought after in Vienna, America – everywhere.

Libby has a quality that you very rarely find but I don't think that she could compete against the Asian youngsters. Their technique is extraordinary. I had one Asian girl who played the Bartók concerto. When we met, I noticed how tiny her hands were but she played without a note out of place. Libby doesn't play like that, but what she does is to engage with the audience. I saw her at a concert in London and when she was coming up to a difficult part, she turned to the audience and said, 'I'm praying! I'm praying!' Just like that – in the middle of the piece. People don't do that – but she does. It's infectious. She is fantastic and people love her.

Libby was always saying that she wanted to play something with me and, one time when she was coming to Melbourne, I suggested that we play the Mozart *Sinfonia Concertante* for violin and viola. Strangely enough, Mozart wrote the two parts in different keys and Libby insisted that I play in D instead of E flat because that's how Mozart originally wrote it. I agreed and we were fine until we came to the cadenza where the viola answers the violin. Libby went off like a rocket and I struggled to catch up and played the whole thing in E flat. Every note was completely wrong and there we were in Melba Hall. Libby laughed and said, 'Let's do it again!' We did and it was fine, and the audience loved it. Some people would faint if that happened to them but Libby laughed, I laughed and we just did it again.

Another past student of mine who has done really well is conductor Warwick Stengards. His father is Swedish but Warwick is as Ocker as you can get. We were close friends at the Conservatorium. He was a gifted violinist, but was never going to make it as a soloist and only got through his exam because I chose his pieces for him. I was good at that. I knew that a concerto he was planning to play wouldn't suit him and found him *Reverie et Caprice* by Hector Berlioz instead. Warwick played it well and passed.

Warwick is, in my view, one of the most gifted of all Australian conductors. You can give him ten scores of contemporary music and he can do it like that – no problem! The ABC uses him a lot for modern music. He is especially good with opera and understands how it works. He and his Hungarian wife and three children live in Vienna, where he was assistant GMD at the Volksoper for four years before being appointed chief conductor at the Luzerne Theater and the Schlossorchester Schönbrunn. He is hugely successful.

When one of my students, Catherine Kaleski – also a good friend of Warwick's – needed a viola, I suggested that we get one from Sotheby's in London. I explained that it was a complete pig in a poke but that I had a feel for a decent instrument and it wouldn't cost too much. She agreed to give it a go, and I started looking in the Sotheby's catalogues. I found a Craske viola and Cathy put in a postal bid for it and actually got it. Sotheby's would have parcelled it up and sent it, but Warwick happened to be in London at the time and offered to bring it back. He waltzed into Sotheby's, signed for the viola and took it away with him. The next thing, my sister-in-law in London, Gill Rosefield, rang and said, 'Chris, who is this Warwick Stengards? He came to my flat in shorts, t-shirt and thongs, with a viola in a brown paper bag, and was drinking beer out of a bottle!' How that viola arrived in one piece I'll never know, but Cathy loves it to this day.

Another of my viola students who has done extremely well is Nicolette Fraillon.[39] She is ambitious and brilliant. She is now the conductor of the Australian Ballet. We have always been close but I don't see much of her and she is often away with the ballet. But she did help me out when I was sick. I had a Doctors' Orchestra concert coming up in Sydney and called her and said, 'Nicky, I have cancer'. 'What do you want me to do?', she asked. I said, 'Conduct the concert for me'. She did it and she was marvellous.

At that time, she was in Canberra as Director of the School of Music. She had applied even though she was convinced that she wouldn't get the job. They invited her for an interview and asked her for her impressions of the School. She thought she had nothing to lose and told them that it was a 'shit place', run badly and needed loads of work. They loved it! All their other interviewees had said that it was a wonderful place and how they really wanted to work there. Nicky got the job and after five years was offered the Australian Ballet in Sydney. She was into her third marriage by that time and had a couple of kids. I said to her, 'Nicky, what about your husband?' She said, 'He'll have to put up with it. My career comes first. He either comes with me or he doesn't.'

Nicky's husband was Dutch and had a good job in Canberra, which he gave up when they moved. I think he worked at the ABC for a while in Sydney but the marriage broke up very quickly, as I suspected it might. Nicky loves her children and her husband, but that's the way she is. To me, she is wonderful and I'm very fond of her.

There was a competition for conductors in Holland and Nicky won it. Hiroyuki Iwaki was one of the judges. There were six finalists and the other five were all Europeans. Nicky said that they treated her like the tea-lady but she won and beat them all. The panel was very taken with her. She stayed on in Holland for a while, as she was offered the job of conducting the Dutch Ballet. She learned an interesting lesson there. When she was rehearsing, she tended to swear when things were not working well. Nothing serious, but enough for the leader of the orchestra to talk to her. 'You're a talented woman', he said, 'so you don't need to swear and the orchestra doesn't like it. We know what you're saying because we all speak English. Don't do it. It's unnecessary and it doesn't help your cause.' He was right, in that women have a hard time making headway as conductors. Nicky never swore again in rehearsals.

One of the many great contemporary musicians who came to the Conservatorium while I was there was the British composer, Sir Michael Tippett. I had first met him many years before in England, when the quartet I played with in London was asked by the BBC to record a work of Tippett's. He used to come to rehearsals and tell us what he wanted. He was very nice to us and everything went well. There are people, my son Ben among them, who think that he is a better composer than Britten. I especially love his *Child of Our Time*.

Tippett came to the Conservatorium to give a series of talks to the students. We were talking one day and Tippett said that Music students should all take a one-year course on learning to play contemporary music, as often they are asked to make sounds that are very different from conventional music. I thought that this was rubbish, as I have played a lot of contemporary music. Always at the beginning there is an explanation of what the different signs mean and how to play them. I never came across one that I couldn't play immediately. So I said what I thought, and Tippett yelled, 'Bullshit! Bullshit!' I was thoroughly put in my place. I didn't remind him of our earlier meeting when we had no difficulty playing his music.

I certainly had a number of challenges when I was at the Conservatorium, because if someone came along and said they wanted to do the Ravel piano concerto, for example, I just did it. The only thing I shied away from was opera, but there were others on the staff happy to do that with the students, which was great.

When I retired from the Conservatorium, my friend Miki Pohl suggested that I join Probus and go along to the University of the Third Age (U3A). I did go to Probus for a while but, apart from one session on whiskey which involved a deal of tasting, the talks didn't really interest me. The U3A had a small orchestra of about sixteen members. Their conductor was ill and I was asked to take it on. After about a year, we had forty players and when I left after ten years, they were full! It was a marvellous crowd, they loved it and so did I.

Ron Davey and the Tiverton Youth Orchestra at the Albert Hall

After I took up the position at the Conservatorium, I used to go back to England regularly and would always catch up with Ron Davey. He had this dream that one day the orchestra would play at the Albert Hall. I told him that he was crazy. 'Ron', I said, 'you can't, you just can't. It would cost thousands.' Strangely enough his dream came true and it all came about through Libby Wallfisch. She was going to England in 1976 to perform in a series of concerts and, at my suggestion, Ron invited her to be guest soloist at his annual celebrity concert. She was Elizabeth Hunt then and Ron made all the arrangements through her agent, Barbara Graham.

Ron mentioned his secret ambition to Barbara and, to his astonishment, she organised a meeting between him and Miss Herrod, the manager of the Albert Hall. He went to London to see her and she was captivated by him. She offered him the Hall at a greatly reduced fee on an afternoon when there was nothing else on. She thought that he was marvellous and was very taken with the idea of the Youth Orchestra's playing there. He promised her that he would get the whole of Tiverton to come.

The story of this unknown orchestra with an amateur conductor coming from a tiny town in Devon attracted international media attention. That month happened to be Ron's sixty-fifth birthday and all the past members of the Tiverton Youth Orchestra were invited to come and play at the Albert Hall to celebrate. To my great delight, I was able to be there too. The concert was a huge hit; everybody loved it and it was televised. Ron had everybody singing along to the *Pomp and Circumstance March* at the end, and he gave a speech about always wanting to play at the Albert Hall because the greatest violinists had played there, including Kreisler, Jascha Heifetz and Albert Sammons. The only thing that went wrong was that Ron brought the wrong trousers. They were too loose and he had to keep pulling them up, but people thought it was funny. When he presented Ron with gifts from the orchestra at the end of the concert, Viscount Amory joked that he hoped they included braces![40]

Poor Ron missed all the television coverage of the concert and speeches shown later that evening, because the buses from Tiverton broke down on the motorway going home. But he did get a wonderful letter from Albert Sammons' daughter, who was thrilled that Ron had mentioned her father when so many had forgotten him.

Ron was an extraordinary man. He never thought anything was impossible, even if other people thought that he was crazy. Another example of this was his determination to take the Youth Orchestra to Germany. He felt that the only way to build friendships between countries was for the young to meet each other. In spite of some local disapproval (bad memories of the war still lingered), he took the orchestra a number of times to Hofheim and, in return, Tiverton hosted visits from the Hofheim Akkordeon Orchester. This exchange led to the two towns being twinned. Annette and I and the children were in Europe once when the Tiverton Youth Orchestra was in Hofheim and Simon and I joined them for a few days.

Ron was given the MBE for his contribution to Tiverton, which he thoroughly deserved. It stands for Member of the British Empire, as opposed to the OBE, the higher award, which is the Order of the British Empire. Ron used to refer to the OBE as 'Other Buggers' Efforts' and the MBE as 'My Bloody Effort'. There's a grain of truth in that. MBE people are often those who work on the coalface. What Ron did for music, for Tiverton, still goes on.

A friend of mine once told me, years after the event, that a group of people got together to put in an award for me for my years of work with community orchestras and music camps. They didn't realise that I wasn't an Australian citizen and wasn't eligible. I said never mind, maybe the Queen will give me a knighthood.

Music lessons

> Annette: Two of our children, Ben and Simon, are very fine musicians but Simon doesn't play our sort of music, which wasn't easy for us or for him and he hasn't always felt accepted. Just to give an example, Simon insisted on practising with an amplifier, which was impossible inside the house where we string players were all practising quietly. Simon eventually went to practise at the home of a friend who also played guitar. Ben played cello and piano, of course. He filled the house with the sort of music we loved. Both Ben and Simon became professional musicians. This may sound as though Naomi is left out, but she's always been a terrific listener and played violin and viola. She never had the passion for music that the boys did. She once wrote an autobiography in which she said, 'If all else fails, I might have to become a professional musician', which I thought was terribly funny. At the time, she had no idea how hard it is.

Simon is self-taught on the guitar. Annette would find him teachers to help him but he wouldn't go. He would say, 'I don't need lessons. I know what I'm trying to do.' What he has achieved – and people who know his music say that he is brilliant – he has done himself. With Ben, I first realised he had a talent for the piano when we were in England on my sabbatical. Ben was seven and very taken with the music from The Sting. There was a piano where we were staying and he sat down and played it right though. It was amazing. He had an instinctive understanding of the piano and advanced very quickly when he started having lessons. He would play for hours and hours. He chose to go to the Victorian College of the Arts for his secondary education and was later accepted at the Juilliard. One of his greatest teachers was Dorothy Taubman, an eccentric Jewish woman living in New York.

> Annette: Ben was like a sponge, always looking for recordings and bringing them home and playing things to us that we would never have known otherwise. He would play with us if we wanted him to, but I don't think we did a lot of music together. I usually practised when the kids weren't there and feel it was a bonus that I could do it at all.

There has been an enormous change in parents' approach to children's music lessons. I used to drop Naomi off at the teacher's place, have a nice run around the park or something and then go and pick her up an hour later. Other parents did the same. These days, especially with parents from Asian backgrounds, it is very different. The mother goes to the lesson, takes notes, listens intently. When the kids get home, their mothers make sure that they do exactly as the teacher said. These children work extremely hard and play extremely well and tend to dominate the little music competitions in Melbourne. A number of my friends give private music lessons to young people and they all comment on this phenomenon.

It really amuses me when people talk about the lineage of their music teachers. One of my dearest friends, Ron Farren-Price, once told me that he was extremely proud of the fact that he could go back to Beethoven through his teacher, the great pianist Claudio Arrau. Arrau studied with so and so, who was a pupil of Liszt, who was a pupil of someone else, and so you eventually get back to Beethoven. And I said to Ron, 'Well, your worst pupils can say the same thing!' He was a bit taken aback but had to admit that I was right. I pointed out that my own teacher, Henry Holst, studied with Fleishman and through him I can go back to Paganini. Here in Melbourne, Ben had a teacher called Semetzki. Originally from Russia, he was taught by Emil Gilels, who, with Sviatoslav Richter, was considered one of the great Russian pianists of the twentieth century. So it's not so hard to go back to the giants.

Great disasters of the world

My daughter, Naomi, used to buy these silly American magazines called *Great Disasters of the World*. She was astonished when she found a story about me in one of them. 'Hey Dad, you're in there!', she said. 'I can't be.' But I was! What happened was this: when I was teaching at Melbourne University, the Music Department and the Melbourne Symphony Orchestra were linked through the Lady Northcote Trust and the Myer Foundation. The University and the Orchestra would decide on four concerts to be held in the Myer Music Bowl – two on Saturdays, two on Wednesdays.

This particular year, 1983, they asked me to play the viola solo in *Harold in Italy* by Berlioz. Paganini was a great friend and admirer of Berlioz, who played both the viola and violin, and asked him to write a viola concerto for him. Berlioz was not happy about writing a full viola concerto, so he wrote *Harold in Italy* based on Byron's *Childe Harold*. It's a symphony with a big obligato part for the viola.

The guest conductor for this series of four concerts was a Dutchman called Hubert Soudant, and I really didn't like him. He was mean to me and condescending, but quite good with the orchestra and they rehearsed well. I was anxious, as I'm not a big solo player and the Myer Music Bowl is daunting; you can get two or three thousand people there on a hot night.

On the evening of the concert, Annette drove me in. It was incredibly hot, over forty degrees even in the early evening. The sky had this red glow, it was looking a strange night. The concert began with an overture and I was waiting in the dressing rooms, underneath the stage. I was so nervous that I had taken a couple of beta blockers so I could control my bow. I played a few notes and noticed that the pitch on my viola was unusually high. The heat can have that effect on stringed instruments. Eventually the orchestra manager came in and said, 'You're on!' And off I went.

The first movement, the longest, was good; I played well, I was OK. The second movement, the *March of the Priests*, is a beautiful piece and the viola has some lovely parts ending with a series of slow, easy goes into arpeggios. Suddenly, as I was playing the arpeggios, there was a roar like you wouldn't believe. An enormous roar – and the Bowl was filled with what we thought was dust, as if a massive dust storm had erupted. The harp nearly blew over, the stands blew over, the conductor cried,

'Run, run, everybody run!' As we all grabbed our things, there was an announcement: 'Go home. Victoria is on fire.' It wasn't dust – it was ash!

Annette and I went to a friend's house and watched what was happening on television. It was a terrible disaster, afterwards known as Ash Wednesday. Bizarrely, this American magazine included in their list of great disasters the fact that the viola player couldn't finish his piece in the concert.

That was the second concert of the four, and I asked Soudant if he could programme me in again and let me finish the piece. To my annoyance he said no, that as far as he was concerned, the programme ended there. The ABC rang and apologised for not repeating the concert as Soudant didn't want to and only gave me half the fee! Actually that's not quite true – it's just that the fee was so small it felt like only half.

I was once at a concert in the Wigmore Hall in London with Miki Pohl, listening to a French quartet playing Beethoven. In the middle of this beautiful, slow movement a flunky from the back of the hall marched up the aisle, *clomp, clomp, clomp*. The quartet stopped in amazement, as the man stood there and shouted, 'EVERYONE LEAVE THE HALL IMMEDIATELY! GO TO CAVENDISH SQUARE AND YOU WILL BE TOLD WHEN THIS CONCERT WILL RECOMMENCE.' There wasn't any panic, people just got up and filed out. Soon there were sniffer dogs and police everywhere, sirens blaring and they even blocked the street. Apparently the Turkish ambassador was present and they had received a bomb threat from the Kurds. The ambassador was whipped away immediately. It all turned out to be a hoax, but in London you must react to threats because if it wasn't a hoax, the consequences would be terrible. We didn't hang around. Miki said that there was no way the concert would restart and we went off and had a marvellous meal.

The Chamber Strings of Melbourne

The Chamber Strings of Melbourne was founded by Dr Alexandra Cameron in 1980, a remarkable woman who has dedicated her adult life to youth and music. She's 101 now. I was first invited to conduct them in 1983 at the recommendation of their first conductor, Harry Hutchins. He took them for three years and I have worked with them ever since, apart from a short break when Spiros Rantos took over before leaving

Melbourne for Brisbane. Dr Cameron was impressive to work with. As she grew older, she had problems with hearing and seeing but never with thinking.

We did a lot of overseas tours to Europe, which Cam and I would plan together. When we decided where we wanted to go, we would get in touch with local people and work with them. Cam kept every little detail in her head, down to the most mundane. On our trip to Vienna in 1998, for example, we were going to give a concert in someone's home on the outskirts of the city before heading back to the centre to go to the opera. She rang me before we left Melbourne to tell me that as there would not be enough time to go back to our hotel before we went to the opera, so the students would have to go to the toilet before getting on the bus. 'But Cam', I said, 'there'll be toilets at the opera'. 'There won't be time, there won't be time', she insisted, 'and there will be queues'. I confess that I said sarcastically, 'Cam, do you want me to stand by the door of the bus and make sure everyone goes to the toilet?' 'Yes', she said, 'that's your responsibility'.

As it happens, that trip to Vienna was one of our most memorable. Together with hundreds of young people from good orchestras around the world, we took part in the twenty-seventh International Youth and Music Festival. Cam and I were pleased but not surprised when we won our section – we knew that we were good. One of the pieces we played was Sculthorpe's *Port Essington*. What came as a shock was winning the Mayor of Vienna's Special Prize for the whole competition. I didn't think we had hope of that, as there was a brilliant orchestra from Spain and another good one from the UK. They both won their sections, too, but the overall prize for best performance came to us.

One of the officials referred to the Chamber Strings of Melbourne as an orchestra of music students. Oh no, I told him, only a couple are music students and they are not our best players. He was shocked when I said that most of the performers were still at school and the rest were at university and studying all sorts of subjects but not music. Well, you must rehearse a lot, he said. Not really, I told him, only two-and-a-half hours on Sunday mornings. This would be unthinkable in Europe but I believe that it contributed to our spontaneity and enthusiasm.

When the result was announced, all the members of the orchestra were given a medal and Dr Cameron and I were given some beautiful pieces of crystal. The hotel staff offered to wrap them and post them to Melbourne for us. When Cam demurred, they were put out. 'Madame, we send things all over the world', they said. They wrapped the pieces of crystal in newspaper and put them in a cardboard box; when they arrived in Melbourne, they were smashed to smithereens. Our other disappointment was not getting any acknowledgement when we got home, even though we informed the Victorian Government, the Melbourne City Council and the newspapers. Can you imagine the excitement if we had been a sporting team and not a small youth orchestra?

Five years ago, in 2005, we went to Russia, Finland, Estonia, Denmark and Holland. As St Petersburg is a sister city to Melbourne, Cam got in touch with the Mayor's office in the city to let them know. Before we left, we were invited to the saddest reception I have ever attended. We were welcomed by the Deputy Mayor, who didn't even know who we were. We were offered sickly soft drinks and biscuits and given show bags to hand out in Russia. They contained out-of-date brochures on Melbourne, a plastic biro stamped with the words 'Greetings from Melbourne', and a tiny koala with a sticker on its bottom saying 'China'.

The day after our concert in St Petersburg, we were invited to a reception in one of the palaces. It was a wonderful, wonderful occasion. The palace was small but exquisite and there was abundant champagne and soft drinks and beautiful little things to eat. The Australian Consul was present and gave a speech about trade that was particularly boring, so when I was invited to speak too I decided to say something more meaningful. 'St Petersburg is very special to me because so many of my heroes were here', I began and went on to say who they were. I talked about Lev Pulvar, who taught violin at the St Petersburg Conservatory at the turn of the nineteenth century, a great teacher enticed to the city from Hungary by the Tsar. One of his students was Efrem Zimbalist, who was among the most famous violinists of his day. Another great musician and teacher at the Conservatory was Leopold Auer, also Hungarian, and he was invited to the Conservatory by its founder, the pianist Anton Rubinstein. Other students came from all over Russia, a number from Odessa, a beautiful port on the Black Sea which had a huge Jewish community.

And I talked about other outstanding musicians who lived, studied and worked in St Petersburg – it was the place to be – and finished by saying how good it was to bring our little orchestra from Melbourne and that we came with love and friendship. It was a good speech and was enthusiastically applauded. Afterwards I realised how ironic it was that every person I had mentioned was Jewish and yet Jews weren't allowed in the holy city of St Petersburg. The Tsar was deeply anti-Semitic but Pulvar persuaded him to grant a number of fine Jewish musicians a dispensation as long as they came with one parent.

In 2010, the Chamber Strings celebrated its thirtieth anniversary with a concert in the Melbourne Town Hall for which Dr Cameron put together a display of memorabilia including old programmes and correspondence. It was quite an occasion. The concert was conducted partly by me, aged eighty, partly by John Hopkins, aged eighty-four, and partly by Spiros Rantos. It was quite a celebration of old age, as the orchestra was still managed by Cam who was 100. This was her last concert before retiring. There were about eighty in the orchestra that day, current and past players, all strings. Some hadn't seen each other for ten years or more. Most of them had been in the orchestra with me, and we had done tours together, so we knew each other well. It was a wonderful afternoon and extremely successful.

Australian Doctors' Orchestra

At the annual Mount Buller Chamber Music Summer School in January nearly twenty years ago, Miki Pohl came up to me and said that he wanted to start an Australian Doctors' Orchestra. When I asked him what he had in mind, he said, 'I want you to conduct it'. 'But I'm not a doctor', I protested. 'You'll be the only one', he replied and I said, 'OK, when do we start? Next year?' 'No, now!', he said. I was shocked until I heard that he already had seventy-four willing players. We gave our first concert later that year with William Kimber, a general practitioner, playing the Beethoven Piano Concerto No. 3 in C. He played well and, at my suggestion, the money went to the Multiple Sclerosis Society in honour of Jacqueline du Pré.

Initially we gave our concerts in Melba Hall at Melbourne University. It was refurbished about halfway through my tenure and made into what it is today. It's a wonderful hall to play in. I love it. It holds about 200 people, but as we attracted more and more people to our concerts we had to look for somewhere bigger and moved to the Iwaki Auditorium, which takes about 450.

I tell the orchestras I work with that there are more adventurous conductors than me. I am not adventurous and have too much respect for song music to allow myself to do it with amateurs. I have friends who say that they're going to do Mahler No. 4, but I wouldn't touch it with a 50-foot pole. I couldn't do it justice with an amateur orchestra. Other people don't agree with me, but I feel that I couldn't realise the symphony as I would want to, so I don't do it.

There is a great connection between medicine and music. When I was at the University, we offered a music course for students in other disciplines. The only stipulation was that students had to play in the orchestra. We got more medicos than students from other subjects. I used to audition them and, if I thought they were good enough, they could have lessons as well.

The best known example of a musical doctor is Albert Schweitzer. He was a great organist, a great Bach scholar and wrote a two-volume book on his life and work. Another example is Fritz Kreisler, who took a degree in medicine in his twenties when he was already a famous violinist, but I don't think that he ever practised medicine. The other discipline often linked with music is mathematics. Einstein, for example, adored the violin. Because he was so well known, he played with all the best musicians. There is a story about his playing in a quartet with Isaac Stern. He kept getting lost and Stern, exasperated, turned to him at one point and said, 'The trouble with you, Albert, is that you can't count!'

I've had some wonderful experiences with the Australian Doctors' Orchestra. We've played in Sydney, Brisbane – all over the place. The secret to good programming is to work with the material you've got. I've made mistakes. There was an overture called *Colas Breugnon* by Kabalevsky and I thought, we'll do it, it'll be fine. But it was not only hard for them, it was hard for me as well and anyway, they didn't like it.

The audience seems to enjoy it if I chat before and after concerts, about this and that. The person who took over from me when I was sick was Keith Crellin, from South Australia, a good friend and fine conductor. I had put his name forward. He was there for the last concert that I was well enough to conduct and I said to the audience, 'I don't know who is conducting next year. The committee has given me a list of fifty conductors and they are all dead.' And Miki Pohl said, 'Keith Crellin's not dead!' And I said, 'He's not dead?' And I carried on like this and later worried that I might have offended him, but he didn't seem to mind.

With the Corpus Medicorum, I advised Phillip Antippa that it should be a Beethoven orchestra and not spread to the big symphonies of Tchaikovsky, Sibelius, Rachmaninov and Mahler. But the orchestra's grown. It has a lot of strings and really excellent wind, though it doesn't have tubas, trombones and double percussion and all those extras that you can have, so to me it's still a Beethoven orchestra.

In his annual concerts with the orchestra, Keith Crellin likes to expand the repertoire. He's done Brahms's No. 1, Sibelius's No. 2 and this year wants to do Shostakovich's No. 5, which I wouldn't go near – it's not me. It's not that the work isn't great; it's just not me. Phillip thinks that I'm too safe. The last concert that I did was all Beethoven.

I love an orchestra the size of the Doctors' Orchestra. Bigger than that and it becomes unwieldy. With contemporary composers like Shostakovich, you have to have timpani plus three other percussion players, a harp, a piano – and that's just a start. On top of that, you need three bassoons, a counter-bassoon, four trumpets and three trombones. It's a great challenge for the orchestra, of course, and Phillip likes it, but for me, it's too much.

Another conductor took over from me when I was very sick, too sick to conduct any more. He has done works that I wouldn't touch, and that's fine. If I have a weakness, then perhaps it's that I haven't given orchestras that sort of challenge. Over the years I have told them that if they want to do a piece that I don't want to do, then they must get another conductor.

A consideration of composers

Ben Britten once said that after the Purcell era in the second half of the seventeenth century, there was a dearth of British music for about 300 years – though strangely enough, London was one of the musical centres in the world. Everyone went there: Beethoven, Mozart, Haydn, Handel. It was because of the Royal Society and the number of concerts and orchestras. Music flourished but it was the music of other countries – of Germany, France, Hungary, Italy, Austria. England at the time of Purcell had probably the best musical tradition in Europe, with people like William Byrd and Orlando Gibbons, then it was as if a curtain came down on English expressive music.

The great classical romantic period of Haydn, Mozart, Beethoven, Schubert, Schumann and Brahms didn't produce English composers, though there was a lot going on musically. Then in the nineteenth century we get Edward Elgar, and interestingly enough his first success was in Germany not England. He loved living there and his *Enigma Variations* were first performed there. He wrote a lot of studies and salon pieces for the fiddle because he played himself – pieces that everybody knows, now like *Salut d'Amour*.

Even though England was slow to appreciate Elgar, towards the end of the nineteenth century there was an enormous swell of pride in English music. Hubert Parry was writing stirring pieces like *Jerusalem* and *Blessed Pair of Sirens* and with the turn of the century we have Ralph Vaughan Williams, for me an even greater giant than Elgar, and Gustav Holst. They studied together at the Royal College of Music and were great friends. Vaughan Williams always showed his new works to Holst and took note of his comments. After them came William Walton and what a composer he was! And there were others, such as Frank Bridge who taught Benjamin Britten.

There were great composers in Europe, of course. France, for example, had Debussy and Ravel, the Hungarians had Kodály and Bartók, the Austrians had Mahler, the Finns had Sibelius, the Czechs had Janácek and Dvorák, the Russians had Stravinsky, Shostakovich, Prokofiev, Rachmaninov. Most people thought the English composers didn't compare but they were actually very skilled, even the minor ones like Eric Coates who inspired listeners to the wireless during the war with *The Dambusters March* and *In Town Tonight.* He was wonderful.

I often wonder what of lasting value has been written in the past few decades compared to the earlier period. Phillip Glass would be one of the best and of course there's Peter Sculthorpe, whose music I love but is it on a par with Bach or Beethoven? My feeling is that there has been a real decline in great composing. Looking back over the twentieth century, to me one of the most outstanding of all was Alban Berg. His *To the Memory of an Angel* is, to my mind, the greatest violin concerto of the period, his *Wozzeck* and *Lulu* the finest operas. He studied with Schoenberg – another giant – and together with Anton Webern was part of the second Viennese school. And we mustn't forget Pierre Boulez. Nothing escaped his ear, nothing. He thought that his piece

Le Marteau sans Maître would rival Schoenberg's *Pierrot Lunaire,* but who plays it now?

One of the great figures linking the nineteenth and twentieth centuries is the French musician Nadia Boulanger. Just as Vaughan Williams went to Holst, Stravinsky consulted her, as did Bernstein, Copland, Gershwin and Sculthorpe, among others. She was there for everybody. Bernstein once told me of Nadia, 'She knew everything! She'd say, "I wouldn't do it that way", and I didn't.' As well as composing and teaching, she was the first woman to conduct the major orchestras in Europe and America. She was a colossus.

The question you have to ask yourself is this: in twenty years time, is anyone going to play Stravinsky? Yes. Is anyone going to play Bartók? Yes. Sibelius? Yes. James Brett? Górecki? I wonder. You can write anything these days, without form or harmony. That sort of music is hard to conduct. David Porcelijn, the Dutch conductor in Tasmania, is terrific with contemporary music. He knows what he's doing, he's as clear as crystal, but many conductors, including myself, can't do it justice.

Composers can have a tough time, even the giants like Bartók. He was very sick with leukaemia in the last few years of his life, living in America and short of money. Boosey and Hawkes, the big English music publishers, held the rights to his work and only published bits and pieces. Bartók was the greatest composer of his time apart from Stravinsky and yet they said that his music wasn't selling. Britten fell out with them for similar reasons.

Bartók was too proud to accept financial help, so his friends – particularly his Hungarian friends, like Serge Koussevitsy – organised commissions and paid him well. Koussevitsy commissioned the Concerto for Orchestra for the Boston Symphony Orchestra and this became Bartók's most popular work. Sadly he died within a year of its first performance in 1944.

The big Jewish migration to America in the twentieth century had a big impact on music there, especially with musicals. Think of Bernstein's *West Side Story* and *Candide.* Marvellous stuff – so much better than his more serious music, which nobody listens to. There was also Irving Berlin, Frederick Loewe, Gershwin and Aaron Copland. And then, writing music for films is a whole new genre.

Masterclasses

Given the right way, masterclasses can be wonderful. Watch Paul Tortelier, the great cellist, on YouTube. He understands that you can't make a cellist out of someone in five minutes. The best you can do is to encourage them and make them feel that what they are doing is OK, and guide them in a musical way – sometimes in a technical way but always in a delicate, gentle way. The worst thing is to jump in with both feet and say, 'What you're doing is wrong. Do it this way.' I've often seen that happen and it's devastating.

A fantastic viola player called Wolfram Christ gave a masterclass at Melbourne University when I was there.[42] One of the women students played eight bars of a piece for him and he then replayed them brilliantly. Every time she played it again, it was worse, because there was no way that she could do it like him. In the end, he got fed up and called the next person in and the first student went away demoralised. The professional player ruined that class because he could have said, 'What you're doing is fine, but if you try it this way it will be better'. Everyone has got their own way of playing in the end and each is valid. It doesn't mean that what the student was doing wasn't musical – she loved music – but he destroyed her in twenty minutes and I don't like to see that.

Tortelier had a way of nurturing young musicians. He made them feel good. Every time they played again, they played a bit better because he was drawing it out of them. He's one of the greatest teachers I have ever seen, very different to some famous musicians who insist on students playing pieces that they – the master – know well and can use to show off their skills to the audience. That's not teaching; it's entertainment. It's also about lording it over inexperienced players rather than getting on their wavelength and helping them.

Annette went to masterclasses with Pablo Casals in Zermatt and in Prades. Jacqueline du Pré was at Zermatt too, and she would throw herself into music and get terribly emotional. Casals sat back and beamed. One or two people there were irritated by this and said, 'Maestro, you are the greatest cellist in the world and here you have a young girl of fifteen and you say nothing!' 'I don't want to spoil this moment', he said. 'Why put an old head on young shoulders? It's just wonderful to hear her youthfulness and exuberance. I love it, I love it, let's enjoy it for what it is.'

John Barbirolli was the same. Jackie played the Elgar with him at the Albert Hall. I was there and I wept. To see this older man and young person make such music together was deeply moving. I heard that some people said Jackie was too emotional with the music, with her body language and everything, and wanted Barbirolli to rein her in but he wouldn't. He said, 'If you can't be emotional at nineteen, when can you be?'

It wasn't easy to get into a Casals masterclass. You had to book through his friend and fellow cellist Rudolf von Tobel. Casals was very old by this stage and his hands were too weak to tune the cello – von Tobel did all that for him, but he still played. When Annette went to von Tobel, he asked, 'Why should you play to the master?' Annette wasn't one of the best students and von Tobel thought that he was protecting Casals but Annette persisted and eventually had her turn. She played a Saint-Saëns concerto and found Casals inspirational. He was an extraordinary musician. The great Fritz Kreisler called him 'the monarch of the bow'.

Many musicians coming from overseas give masterclasses here in Australia. I remember saying to one friend, 'Masterclasses are the easiest thing that you do in your life, aren't they?' 'Money for jam', she replied. 'I work with the student. I demonstrate. The audience is there, they say, "Isn't this wonderful!" and the next day I'm gone.' It's true that the young musician has this short inspiring time but then they are left hanging. They go back to their teacher and say, so and so told me to do it this way, and the teacher will have no idea what the student is talking about. It upsets the routine and they don't like it.

I myself have done many masterclasses and I think I do them well, though that would be a matter of opinion. In my masterclasses, the audience is usually small – the people involved and their friends. With celebrities, of course, it's a much bigger deal and clearly some are astonishing, but in my view many of the big players don't all do masterclasses well. My dear friend Hartmut Lindemann, for example, is a brilliant artist but gets side-tracked in masterclasses. Isaac Stern was outstanding in masterclasses, as you can see in his film *From Mao to Mozart*, which depicts his work in China,[43] but players with a big ego like the Polish violinist Henryk Szeryng are the worst.

Szeryng gave a masterclass at the Conservatorium once and I had to find the right students to work with him. One was a wonderful violinist called Cathy Weiss. Cathy decided that she was going to play Mozart for Szeryng and was a few bars into it when he picked up his fiddle and played the whole movement. 'Now you know what it should sound like', he said. She was extremely upset.

There is an art, a real craft in successful masterclasses. You have to make the person feel good and you also have to entertain your audience. The aim is not to destroy, not to make the other player feel that what they are doing is wrong musically, because who are you to say that what they are doing is not musical?

Reflections on conducting

My only experience of conducting before I came to Australia was with the Christopher Martin Orchestra in Edinburgh, when I found that conducting strings came naturally to me. I have enjoyed conducting enormously ever since. The basics with conducting are straightforward, as long as you know your score well and understand the strings. The basics are the number of beats in a bar and where they go; five, for example, can be three and two or two and three – they become subdivisions. It's all very natural, very easy. The other important thing is to learn your score and to understand the strings and what they are doing. I knew all that and felt that I conducted quite well. The big problem for me was the wind instruments. Some of them transpose, and so when you look at the score, what you see is not what you hear.

Many of the great conductors, like Bernstein, play the piano extremely well. I don't, but I haven't found that too much of a drawback. A lot of conductors in the past worked as repetiteurs with the opera.[44] They learned the music very thoroughly that way. Solti is a classic example of a conductor who thoroughly learned his skills in opera houses – in his case, in Germany. It gave him incredible knowledge and expertise and was a tough training ground. Now there are conducting schools all over the world but it's a relatively new thing to learn conducting in that way.

Bernstein has made a DVD in which he talks about conducting. He says that it's not just making the right movements, it's communicating through the music. If you have something to say in the music and can convey it, then maybe you can be a conductor. Good conductors, in my view, also need a strong ego otherwise they can't control the orchestra. As a conductor you must believe in yourself, otherwise the orchestra will kill you; it can suss out a conductor's vulnerability in ten minutes. It's especially important if you are not that good. You've got to trust yourself, believe in yourself, have sufficient ego to carry you otherwise the orchestra is going to ask awkward questions and will not play well for you.

The English Chamber Orchestra, for example, was once rehearsing with a young conductor who got to the end of the first movement of a piece and said, 'I think we'll go through that again'. Emmanuel Hurwitz, the orchestra's famous leader who was very well known in the music scene, asked why. The conductor was nonplussed and couldn't answer. He was using the orchestra to learn the score and they spotted it instantly.

Having played in orchestras, I was always able as a conductor to have a good rapport with the strings. I knew how they ticked. Years ago, conductors had the reputation of being swine even though their work might be extraordinary. The Hungarian, Fritz Reiner, for example, was hated but respected at the same time. Bernstein said that he was a pig of a man but, in the end, his performances were amazing. You might think that you know the score, but Reiner could see things that you never thought of. He's a good example of an autocratic conductor.

Another Hungarian conductor who was deeply unpopular was Georg Széll. Musicians were always telling jokes about each other – viola players in particular came in for a lot of flack. Well, there was a joke going around about Széll, that he died and went to heaven where St Peter told him that he would have to atone for treating his musicians so badly. For his punishment, he was teamed up with a witch of a woman who ordered him around in a most unpleasant way. He couldn't get rid of her. When he saw Herbert von Karajan with Marilyn Monroe on his arm, he complained bitterly, saying that von Karajan was even harder on his musicians than he was and none of them liked him. 'Marilyn Monroe's punishment is nothing to do with you', answered St Peter.

I never played with Széll myself but I did play with Solti, another difficult Hungarian. All these people, however unpleasant, were amazing conductors. The Hungarians have an astonishing musical tradition. At one time, you couldn't walk around London without falling over a Hungarian conductor. All the major orchestras had Hungarian conductors: the BBC had Antal Dorati; George Solti was at Covent Garden; the great István Kertész was at the London Symphony Orchestra.[45] He died tragically young, drowning in the sea in Israel while visiting friends. A great loss. Every Hungarian also talks with reverence of Fritz Reiner. He was a very respected Hungarian conductor, a great chamber music coach and a great musician.

Yehudi Menuhin is one of the most famous men I have known. I loved him as a person and as a musician. He was a great violinist but everybody knows that he was not such a good conductor. I have played with him and know many others who have too, and we all found that he was not well prepared. What saved him was that the orchestra liked and respected him as a human being and played well for him. Perhaps he found conducting difficult.

> Annette: It's an interesting psychological set-up between conductors and players. The players' capacity to find a conductor's vulnerability is like an animal instinct. The relationship between the two can be unhealthy. It's like a school teacher walking into a class, especially one of teenagers. They know when they can get away with something or what that person is going to pick on. Many conductors, however, feel that they have to be separate from the orchestra. There was one conductor at the MSO called Willem van Otterloo, an aristocratic Dutchman, who never saw the players as equals. In contrast, take the young Pascal Tortelier. He used to play in the orchestra and has enormous empathy with the players as musicians, so he doesn't treat himself as apart from them. He makes music with them and relates to them as equals.

Annette and I had a good friend, Nelli Shkolnikova, probably the greatest female violinist Russia has had.[46] She lived in Melbourne for many years and died here last year. She was doing a recording of Tchaikovsky with the London Symphony Orchestra, with a conductor who shall be nameless. She was staying will Annette's sister Gill and we were there at the rehearsal. At the first break, Nelli came to us in distress and said, 'Chris, I don't know what to do. I am trying, I am trying but this conductor is impossible!' One of the wind players told her that the orchestra was behind her and understood how hard it was. 'Trust me, we are doing our best for you because you are such a great player', he said. The conductor repeated and re-recorded sections that didn't work well and said that it could be pieced together later in the studio and be fantastic – and actually, it was.

I haven't done many recordings myself, other than quite a few broadcast recordings of the Edinburgh String Quartet with the BBC. The Amadeus Quartet was doing hundreds, but we weren't doing any apart from the times we played at the Edinburgh Festival. In those days, companies were very selective whereas now everything is recorded.

I was once asked to do a recording session at Monash University to provide the background music for an advertisement. There was a small viola solo, only about half a minute long. They kept asking me to repeat it and eventually I asked why. 'You're breathing!', they said. So I held my breath and they still weren't happy. Then I asked the woman sitting next to me to play it and she did. 'Thank you', they said, and that was that. Their equipment was so sensitive that it captured me taking a breath before I even played. I don't think that going to such extremes is necessary. I love hearing Casals groan while he plays. I can't imagine *him* doing it again!

Most of my conducting has been in Australia. After Edinburgh, I didn't get back to it until I took up my appointment at Melbourne University. As well as conducting the faculty orchestra, I became involved with the Chamber Strings of Melbourne and the U3A Orchestra. I found that I was fine with conducting. I loved it. One thing I always did was to speak to the audience. It comes easily to me and I think that I have a gift for it. I get up and tell a story about the music or the composers, often it's a bit of nonsense. If the audience responds, I talk more nonsense – usually stories of musicians whom I have known, orchestras that I have played in. I enjoy it and the audience does, too.

I've always had an insight into what I wanted to do with the music I conducted, a sound stage in my head. It's very difficult to achieve that with a poor orchestra. I think that the hardest form of conducting is to work with amateurs and youngsters. First of all, many of them can't play well enough. Second, and this is especially true of amateur orchestras, attendance is unreliable. With the Corpus Medicorum, for example, we had three rehearsals before a concert and there were always people missing. You don't get the full picture until the concert. You put up with the absences because that's the way it works. You can't do anything about it because these are not professional musicians.

A professional conductor doesn't have this situation. Every time you arrive to conduct, the orchestra is complete so your ear always gets the complete sound. The end result is that you always get the balance you want. The sound is balanced because the orchestra itself is balanced. With an amateur orchestra, you don't have that luxury.

As for today's young conductors, they seem to be able to conduct things that would frighten the life out of me. John Hopkins, a good friend, runs a course in conducting at Melbourne University, which is going well. One of his great successes is Benjamin Northey, who works with all the orchestras in Australia as well as overseas. I met Ben in Helsinki studying at the Sibelius School, when I took the Melbourne Chamber Orchestra there. He is getting a lot of work and doing many things for the first time. When you conduct a piece several times, you really settle into your body and your consciousness and can project something special. I think he has that quality.

Another extremely successful Australian conductor is Brett Kelly, who is also principal trombonist with the Melbourne Symphony Orchestra. He does opera, too, as well as a range of works and makes a huge contribution to the Australian music world. Simone Young, however, is undoubtedly the leading Australian conductor.

The Holy Grail for me as a conductor is Beethoven's Ninth Symphony. It's such a momentous work, so much bigger than me. I've done Beethoven's Fourth, Fifth, Sixth, Seventh and Eightth and loved them. The Ninth is a huge leap from there and although I could conduct it, I would feel an imposter. The other thing that terrifies me is opera. I've conducted one or two small oratorios but never done opera and never wanted to.

I once did quite a difficult piece by Vaughan Williams with the Stonnington Symphony Orchestra, called *Job: A Masque for Dancing*. It should actually be done with static characters on stage. We hired a projector from the Melbourne Town Hall and showed Blake's drawings of Job while the music was playing. I adore that music, I think it's Vaughan Williams' greatest work, but many in the orchestra didn't like it.

In my own small way, I wanted to do the best for my music and the best for my players. Reflecting on my work as a conductor, I must admit that amateur orchestras I worked with could have been more challenged with a different conductor. I have tended to be conservative in my choice of music for them, because I think that certain things would be too hard both for them and for me. I didn't take this approach with the younger players at the Chamber Strings of Melbourne, because they needed to be exposed to new and difficult material. I gave them challenges and expected them to rise up and meet them. With amateur orchestras such as the U3A, I've held back because I felt that there were pieces that would be impossible for them and also for me, because it's a symphony orchestra and I am more at home with ensemble work. Another factor is that there are only about twenty-five members of the Chamber Strings and I know them and the repertoire inside out. It's second nature for me to get up and do it.

It's an extraordinary thing for Melbourne to have an event of the quality of the International Chamber Music Competition. There's a considerable amount of money involved and it is an immensely prestigious competition. The judging is extremely difficult and jury members mostly come from overseas. They judge both the trios and quartets, which is extremely difficult because they are different animals. They don't mix. The audience is inevitably biased towards Australians, if there are any competing, and in 2007 there was almost a riot because the Tinalley Quartet didn't get through to the final round. Bill Hennessy was furious, everybody was furious, because they were so impressive.

They immediately entered for the International String Quartet Competition in Banff in Canada, which is a major competition, and gave a small concert at the Melbourne Club before they went. They played a massive piece, the C Sharp Minor Quartet of Beethoven, one of his later quartets, and I told them then that they could win Banff, it was so fantastic. And they did.

Last words

Looking back, I sometimes regret not having been born ten years earlier and maybe meeting the musical giants like Fritz Kreisler and Mischa Elman when they were at their best. As it is, I have met and heard wonderful people including Jascha Heifetz. The opportunity to hear great playing was important to me, and even though it was better for me and Annette and the children to come to Australia, I felt that I missed out on the vibrant musical scene in London. It was a big metropolis, the hub of so many tours. I did go to America during my three years with the Melbourne Symphony Orchestra but such tours were few and far between, whereas in my three years with the Netherlands Chamber Orchestra we went to Greece, Israel, France, Germany and twice to America.

Just before we left England, a friend in the Covent Garden Orchestra invited me to join them for a couple of years. They did the Ring Cycle once a year with people like Solti. I confess that I hesitated. My quartet with Carl Pini, the London String Quartet, broke up when he went to Australia and I was immediately offered a spot with the famous Aeolian String Quartet, and again I had to say no. I found it hard. To play the viola in a quartet can be the greatest joy of all. You immerse yourself in the music without the responsibilities of the first violin. I love being in the middle of the music.

There are so many young quartets out there today and they play so well – they look out for intonation, style, ensemble, beat. The first quartet I ever heard that perfectly represents everything which quartets are striving for today is the Tokyo String Quartet. It was like a perfect circle, like one instrument from top to bottom from back to front. They played from Beethoven's Razumovsky Quartets, where the music flows from one instrument to another. They played it seamlessly. I hate that sort of perfection. My circle has edges. The best performances I have ever heard were from quartets where individual playing was distinctive. The viola in the great Hungarian String Quartet, for example, was famous for his ugly sound and I do think that the viola can be a bit ugly. Mozart, Beethoven and Brahms wrote quartets that allowed the instruments their characters.

I think that the change started with the Amadeus String Quartet. Their intonation and ensemble work were incredible, but at the same time Peter Schidlof, the viola, never played like Norbert Brainin, the first violin. They were not individually matched like the Tokyo; they were completely different and each had his own voice. Sigmund Nissel, for me, was a bit pale but that was him, and Martin Lovett was not the greatest cellist around, but the quartet set standards of playing, especially with Schubert and Haydn, that were unsurpassed at the time. Other quartets around at the time that did have enormous character were the Griller, the Budapest String Quartet, the Hungarian String Quartet and the Quartetto Casals. Much of their playing in recording was not together at all but it didn't matter to them. Their focus was on performing not recording. Interestingly enough, modern recording techniques have spurred a whole new range of quartets.

Seating was always a problem with quartets, which is rarely satisfactorily resolved. If you have the first violin on one side facing the audience, who plays opposite? If it's the viola or second violin, they must face inwards – though I would turn outwards as far as I could to play. The Aeolian Quartet had the best solution. Its second violin, Jimmy Bartlett, was left-handed. The cello sat in the middle. Jimmy was a menace in an orchestra. You had to get out of his way or his bow would get in your eye. In the Edinburgh Quartet, I often sat on the outside with Joan Dickson on the inside next to me.

I have a book on the South Place concerts written by a friend of mine, with lots of historic photographs of chamber music groups.[47] The variations on seating arrangements for quartets are fascinating. It shows the Joachim Quartet, for example, with Joachim on the outside, the cellist next to him, then the viola and the second violin on the outside. The viola player with the Amadeus was always on the outside and the Carl Pini Quartet, with whom I played, also had the viola on the outside.

Conway Hall in South Place, near Holborn, was one of the most interesting concert venues in London and an institution in the music world. Every Sunday without fail for decades, chamber music concerts took place there. I heard some marvellous musicians – the Amadeus String Quartet, the Griller Quartet and the Hungarian Quartet. It was only a small hall but everybody went. It was not as upmarket as the Wigmore Hall but there was always something special. One time there I will never forget was meeting Ralph Vaughan Williams. He was an old man then, with a hearing-aid, sitting with his wife Ursula. I talked to him about the music, which clearly totally absorbed him. He was charming.

Wigmore Hall would have to be my favourite concert hall.[48] The sound is amazing. You hear just as clearly at the back as in the front, but because the floor is flat you can't see much. You sit under this little dome and feel that you're in a music cathedral. It used to be called the Bechstein Hall, because they used Bechstein pianos from the showroom next door, but they changed the name during World War I. They started using Steinways, which is ironic because they are still German pianos.

When I first played at the Wigmore Hall, the artists' room was a mess. There were signed programmes and photographs everywhere – mementoes of everyone who ever played there. It was like an Aladdin's Cave. Our Edinburgh String Quartet programme went up, too. The hall has since been done up by its Australian director, William Lyne. I wonder what has happened to that material? Much of it had been there for decades.

People often ask me which are my favourite quartets. It's a hard question to answer, because there are some really great composers whose quartets

I don't like at all. Mendelssohn is played a lot by modern quartets but I'm not a fan. To me, the music is thick and heavy and scrubbing away. There are some wonderful bits but overall I don't think he mastered quartets. Neither did Schumann, though his are lighter. Both Debussy and Ravel wrote quartets which are fantastic, as did Verdi. His sings away like an opera. The only weakness is the fugue that he wrote at the end. Probably my favourite quartets are the first six by Mozart, even though I prefer Haydn as a composer. I love these quartets which Mozart called his 'children', dedicated to Haydn, their 'father'. What is unusual is that he spent a lot of time on them, whereas he wrote most things very quickly.

There is a wonderful story about Mozart's doing a concert with a female violinist. She asked him to write a sonata for her and he said yes, that it would be in the programme the following day. When she arrived before the concert, there was no music. He sat down and wrote her violin part and played his own, completely from memory.

I don't regret coming to Australia but I do regret the experiences that I missed out on in England and that I couldn't have got anywhere else. On the other hand, I had work at the University that I had never done before and I was involved with the development of chamber music in Melbourne. I would have missed all that if I had stayed in London. I have lived in two worlds.

One of the things I loved about Europe was the ease of travelling. I hated the great distance between Australia and England. It was always a terrible wrench saying goodbye to my mother. She never made it difficult for me to leave, and I never went more than two years without seeing her. We wrote all the time. My father treated my mother badly at times. As a child, I saw him hit her across the room and thought, 'You bastard!' I cried and cried. On my visits home, I would ask, 'How's Dad been?' 'Just the same', she'd say. He died in 1972 and I was glad. He was eighty-two. I was able to bring my mother out to Australia as she could never have come when my father was alive. With hindsight, it's obvious that he was traumatised by the war and probably suffering severe depression.

Dad never talked about the war. He was a machine-gunner, for goodness sake – he must have killed people. They had three men on a machine-gun and his was blown up twice. He said that when he was firing, he would aim low and hope that he never killed anyone. He was haunted by the thought, but as a gunner he must have killed people. He'd tell a few stories about being in the trenches in France, but that was it.

The only time Mum came to visit, she arrived on a Thursday morning. She was really tired when she got off the plane. 'How are you, Mum?', I asked. 'A bit tired, sonny', she said. 'Come back and have a nice bath and a rest.' 'What day is it?', she asked. 'Thursday.' 'I'll be alright till Saturday', she said. And she was. She couldn't get over the habit of a lifetime!

Annette: I think that Chris's parents thought they had struck something a bit different with me. For instance, I had this strange habit of wanting to wash myself every day. They just weren't in the way of it! It was so very English. I was lucky that there was a bath at all, even though it was something of a white elephant.

Chris's father was a product of his wartime experiences. He was sensitive, insecure and rather closed. He loved to go down to his vegetable allotment but was often unable to get there because of rain and bad weather and instead sat bored stiff in his chair. I only knew him like that. I didn't get to know him well, but at least I knew who he was and he knew who I was, and there we were!

Ron Davey lived down the road, a man full of life. He loved young people and with his enthusiasm he started the Tiverton Youth Orchestra. Chris found his way there because he could share the violin story with him. His father didn't think Chris had much of a future because of his results at school. Ron found Chris was obviously talented and his mother was prepared to do whatever Ron suggested to get Chris into college. He himself was a self-taught violinist and his imagination knew no bounds. Nothing was impossible or out of reach – a direct contrast to the thinking in Chris's family.

When she married, Chris's sister Betty lived a bus ride away in Somerset. This was village life, a way of life which offers a sense of comfort, where one lives methodically and a bus timetable sets the tone. It is an unassuming, predictable life.

Chris's mother did come out here once. It was the first time that she'd been on a plane and she came with this tiny little case. It was a wonderful thing to see her here with the kids. She had a great gift for telling stories. Naomi has it too. I was sure that she was going to be the English one among the children and she took herself off to connect with Chris's family but she had no intention of making her home in England. I was very interested in that. She has what I call a 'cottage' outlook. She is so modest in her needs and what she wants out of life. It's so unworldly – it's quite beautiful.

Reaching eighty

Libby Wallfisch told me that if I had a concert for my eightieth birthday, on 13 April 2010, she would come. 'You're not doing a concert without me', she said. I asked her to do the G Major Mozart Concerto and she agreed. 'Anything you want, I will play', she said. I was delighted. So she played the Mozart concerto and she had the audience in the palm of her hands. When she walks on to the stage, Libby says something funny or silly – anything. The audience warms to her immediately. I knew that she would make up her own cadenza in the first movement. Baroque specialists these days don't tend to play cadenzas written by other people; they do their own. This time she was in the middle of her cadenza when she slipped into 'Happy Birthday'. The crowd went wild. Then she added 'For He's a Jolly Good Fellow!'. It all wove together beautifully. It was such a happy occasion.

Carl Pini came especially from Sydney to play in the orchestra for that concert. He said that he would sit in the back row – anything. Of course, I put him in as leader. He also played in the Elgar piece for string quartet and orchestra. My son Ben played a piece that he had composed himself, which was very special.

Normally we have the Doctors' Orchestra concerts in the Iwaki Auditorium which seats 450, but this time we went to the Dame Elisabeth Murdoch Hall which seats 1,000. And we filled it! The hospital was happy, everyone was happy.

There were a couple of other concerts around the time of my birthday. One was with the U3A Orchestra, which I conducted for ten years. I love the people there. Some are in their nineties, others in their eighties and then more still in their seventies. It's quite an orchestra! The other special concert was with the Chamber Strings of Melbourne when it was celebrating its thirtieth anniversary.

So there were these three concerts – the Doctors' Orchestra, the U3A and the Chamber Strings – before I became sick, and I did arrive at eighty, and I did do all those things and it was good.

***

Christopher Martin died on 5 October 2011. In her notice in the Melbourne *Age*, his wife Annette stated, 'For a brief second, the music died'.

Interval

Ben Martin recounts a conversation that he had with his father:

> 'Bit tired of music, you know.'
> 'Surely you mean the music business?'

> 'No – music.'

I was a bit perplexed. Dad was very fond of Rachmaninov's remark that music was enough for a lifetime but a lifetime was not enough for music. Yet here he was, the most sensitive musician I have known, proclaiming that he'd heard enough.

> 'How about Bach?'
> 'Ah, Bach I never tire of.'

> 'Beethoven?'
> 'Get tired of 'im.'

> 'Mozart?'
> 'Him also.'

Perhaps Rachmaninoff was thinking of Bach, too …

Annette playing to Pablo Casals in Zermatt, before she met
Chris. The experience of playing for and with Casals was, she
says, unforgettable.

An ensemble put together by Mischa Kogan to play the Schubert two cello quintet at one of his Soirées Musicales at Coppin Hall, Melbourne. From left to right: Joseph Suk, Len Dommett, Henry Wenig, Annette Martin, Mischa Kogan and Chris Martin. The Soirées Musicales were important in the musical life of Melbourne when the Rosefield sisters were young.

Chris and his mother Sarah standing at the back door of the house his family moved to when he was four and which his parents never left. After moving to Australia, Chris continued to visit his mother every other year.

Chris's mother with her granddaughter, Naomi. After the death of her husband,
Sarah made her only visit to Melbourne and enchanted the children with her stories.

As a teenager in Tiverton, Chris worked in the local lace factory, led the Tiverton Youth Orchestra and studied at the London College of Music.

Chris the young professional musician, on a visit to his parents and sister Betty in Tiverton. As an adult, he lived in a very different world to his family but maintained strong links with his Tiverton home.

Above Chris conducting the Corpus Medicorum concert in 2010.

Below Phillip Antippa, founder and concertmaster of Corpus Medicorum.

Chris and Miki Pohl at the party held to celebrate Chris's seventieth birthday.

The talented and beautiful Rosefield sisters in the mid-1950s: Fay (right), Annette (left) and Gillian (behind). Photo: Athol Shmith.

Benjamin Martin and his father playing together in the early 1980s. Chris and Annette encouraged all three of their children to play instruments and their home was always filled with music.

Simon Martin is a largely self-taught professional musician performing in a very different world to that of his parents.

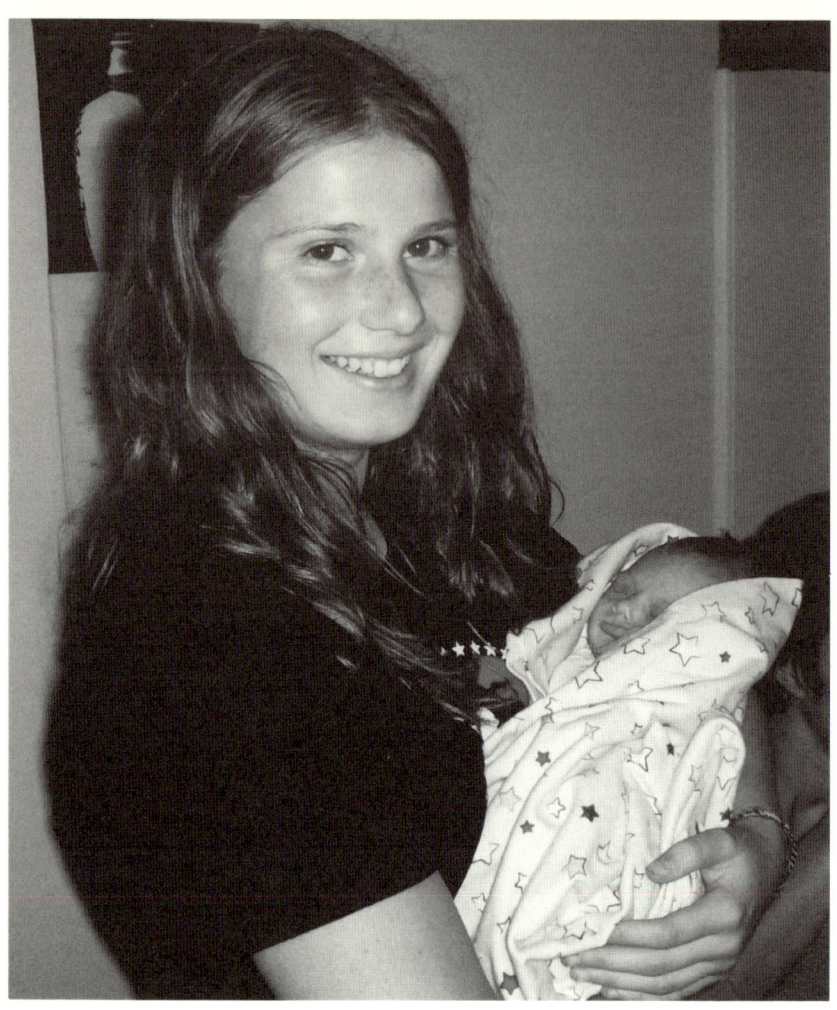

Emma and Edith – Emma was Chris and Annette's only grandchild until Naomi's daughter, Edith, was born in February 2010. In spite of their age difference, Emma, born in 1993, has always cherished her cousin.

Naomi, Annette and Ben.

The Martin family accompanied by Gillian enjoying a holiday in Anglesea in the 1970s. From left to right: Gillian, Simon, Naomi, Ben, Annette and Chris behind.

Benjamin Martin and Hartmut Lindemann enjoy a break from tutoring at the
Mount Buller Chamber Music Summer School in the late 1990s.

Carl Pini and Chris Martin, current and past artistic directors of the Riverina
Summer School which is still held at the Charles Sturt University in Wagga Wagga.

Naomi on her quest for a deeper connection with her father's family, in Somerset with her Aunt Betty.

The last time Chris saw his sister Betty at her retirement home in England she was suffering from dementia and did not experience the usual pain at parting.

Chris rehearsing with the University of the Third Age Orchestra in the church hall in Hawthorn. Photo: courtesy of U3A Hawthorn.

Chris Martin will always be
remembered by his friends and family
for his profound musicality and his gift
for story telling.

PART 2

Memories

Chris's England – Fay Zwicky

Fay Zwicky, Christopher Martin's sister-in-law, is the oldest of the gifted Rosefield sisters and, like Annette and Gillian, an accomplished musician. She settled in Perth in 1960 and held the position of senior lecturer in English at the University of Western Australia until she retired in 1987. She is the author of several books of poetry, a collection of short stories and a collection of essays on literature and survival.

Chris was both simple and complex, growing up a country boy in rural Devon and as an adult finding himself among a very different milieu from that of his childhood. He seems to have fitted in with all kinds of people, having a lot in common with Elgar whose music he loved and served so faithfully. Elgar was also a country boy, who grew up in Worcestershire among the Malvern hills and the Cotswolds, knowing and understanding village people. His father had a shop selling sheet music, pianos and other musical instruments. At sixteen, he became a clerk with a local solicitor, eventually going to London to study law but giving it up for music. At twenty-two, he became bandmaster to the Worcester and Country Lunatic Asylum – coaching the players and writing music for them. Eventually he went to study in Germany. Like Chris, Elgar made that transformation without noticeable strain. Always natural and unspoilt, no matter what the company, and able to get the best results out of often unpromising material, Chris moved between his country origins and life in Australia without compromising his integrity.

It's interesting that so many English composers – like Elgar, Delius and Vaughan Williams – were more appreciated on the Continent than they were in England. Chris, too, was much loved by the orchestras and groups he worked with both in Europe and in England. Chris had a great love for England. I think his England was Edwardian – the England of the World War I poets like Rupert Brook and Wilfred Owen, of the music hall and pantomimes. Never cruel, his awareness was imbued with a melancholy affection that comes across in the English music that he loved so much.

Chris never imposed his ego on either music or friendship. He intuited the music, didn't seek to dominate it, had a genuine feel for its nuances. He also understood folk music and its place in the works of Vaughan Williams, Britten and Delius. His introductions to pieces at his concerts were always informative and well within the range of his audience. He never talked down to people. He was good at getting the tone right.

If Chris had a god, I suppose it was probably the violin and its best exponent, Heifetz. His whole flat was a sort of shrine to the makers of music and of musical instruments; like a reverential archive of those who played and made violins. He loved fine craftsmanship, not only in musical instruments but in everything. He had an instinctive understanding of fine furniture and fine art. It was the same with the makers of Stradivari and Guarneri.

Chris's flat reminded me a bit of the childhood recalled in Keith Richards' autobiography, *Life*. Keith Richards, too, came from humble beginnings in the marshes of Dartford, a Dickensian setting for a poor boy. He had a grandfather, Gus Dupree, quite a character who used to take Keith for walks ending up in the workshop of a big music store where men in brown overalls were busy gluing and mending violins and guitars. Keith fell in love with guitars, just as Chris fell in love with violins. I believe that he once had a violin stolen and it nearly broke his heart, but he never talked about it.

My sister Annette and Chris were both working in the music world when they met, and very much complemented each other. Chris was very good to my family in which there seem to have been a few too many women. My father died at sixty-three and my husband at fifty-seven, so it was good to have Chris for so long. He was a good, kind, generous man. The music was a bonus.

Chris had a great respect for authority, and strong women such as the Queen and Mrs Thatcher. He also adored and admired my mother. The dutiful wife of a doctor, she had been a top-ranking pianist herself and played for the ABC. When I was learning the piano, people used to say that I would never be as good as my mother. Unfortunately, women of her kind sometimes subsumed their talents in marriage and put their energies into their children, but music meant most to her and Chris.

Chris loved arguing with her, typically about the Queen. The more Chris defended the Queen, the more my mother became anti-monarchist; they both loved a bit of pot-stirring. I remember that Chris refused to go and see the Helen Mirren film, *The Queen*, fearing that it would be disrespectful, and he used to stand up for the Christmas speech, much to our amusement. We used to tease him about his devotion to monarchy, but in a good-natured way.

Although Chris and I disagreed from time to time, we were very fond of each other. We had long chats about music and literature. Chris loved Shakespeare, Hardy and Jane Austen, and had a genuine feel for classical literature. He had narrow political sympathies but good instincts and was open to many other influences. Like Elgar and Keith Richards, he grew up in a strange place but, because of his rare, innocent talent, he found much wider horizons. A bit of an autodidact, he became the great, modest person we all loved. An original – a pity that there aren't more like him.

Szymon Goldberg and the Netherlands Chamber Orchestra – Gillian Rosefield

Gillian Rosefield, Christopher Martin's sister-in-law, is a violinist. She was a member of the Netherlands Chamber Orchestra, the Israel Chamber Orchestra and Northern Sinfonia, based in Newcastle-upon-Tyne, and latterly, violinist of the Amati Piano Trio. She lives in London and Hastings.

I was twenty when I met Chris, while I was staying in London with Bruno Schreker (then cellist with the Netherlands Chamber Orchestra (NCO), later cellist with the Oromonte String Trio with Chris as violist). Chris had just left the Edinburgh String Quartet, and together with the second violinist, Anne Crowden, and her five-year-old daughter, Deirdre, was en route to Holland to join the NCO. Chris was a great support to them and very good with Deirdre (now a fine cellist herself). I immediately warmed to Chris, not least because we shared a passion for violins. He had an infinite knowledge of violins and bows and I would forever value his views on these most highly.

I arrived in Holland on 13 April 1959, the day Eduard van Beinum, legendary conductor of the Concertgebouw Orchestra, died. The whole

Dutch nation was in mourning. The young Bernard Haitink, aged twenty-eight, was his immediate successor.

In those days, large-scale symphonic works were favoured. There were few flourishing quartets, and the NCO was one of the first chamber orchestras to be established, with Szymon Goldberg as founder and conductor-director. His performances of Bach Concerti and Haydn C Major were unforgettable in their beauty and purity of style and tone.

When aged only sixteen, Goldberg led the Dresden Philharmonic Orchestra, and at twenty he was invited by Wilhelm Furtwängler to lead the Berlin Philharmonic. He was also in a string trio with composer Paul Hindemith and Emanuel Feuermann.

Goldberg was forced to leave Germany during the Nazi regime, and it was while on a concert tour of Java with pianist Lili Kraus that he was interned by the Japanese for some years. Just before his capture, to avoid confiscation of his Stradivarius, and with his extraordinary knowledge, he chose to take it apart using a knife dipped in butter. He wrapped each of its seventy-three component parts in newspaper and left them on top of a cupboard for a neighbouring doctor to retrieve and keep until after the war. Later, the violin was successfully restored for Goldberg to play again.

I was fortunate that Goldberg finally bowed to the obdurate will of my mother, and agreed to take me on as his only student at that time. (Later, when Chris told Goldberg that he was engaged to my sister Annette, Goldberg's response was, 'Have you met the mother?') Those lessons were to enrich me for life. However, Goldberg saw that I was socially isolated in Amsterdam and with some health problems, so he invited me to join the second violin section of his orchestra. Anne was leader of the section and a fine musician. Musical highlights were concerts in Amsterdam and Germany with Benjamin Britten conducting. (Years later, I would visit Anne in Berkeley, California, where she had established the Anne Crowden Music School.)

There were about twenty-five of us in the NCO, of whom about one-third were British. I was the youngest, greenest and the only Australian. As the NCO was quite chauvinistic (unusual for Holland), you either had to speak Dutch or speak little! Goldberg spoke meticulous Dutch, whereas Anne enjoyed sending the whole thing up with her appalling Dutch. Chris didn't bother to learn Dutch at all. He got by with his usual flair and charm, seemingly immune from these pressures.

Our first tour with the orchestra was to Israel. We sat nervously huddled together before take-off, as neither of us had flown before. The following year, we sailed to the USA on the brand new 38,000-tonne Dutch ship, *Rotterdam*. Towards the end of the ten-day journey, we ran into Hurricane Esther. The seas began to get rough as we played a concert for the passengers. Goldberg turned green. One of the violinists slid out behind a curtain, still playing. Ben Britten's *Pizzicato Polka* sounded more like Morse code. At the height of the hurricane, Chris and I were the only ones on deck; everyone else stayed below, seasick. We stood watching the storm, enjoying the ship's riding high on the waves before plunging to the ocean floor.

This tour was massive – fifty-one concerts in sixty-three days. Chris, with his fund of choice anecdotes, always helped to relieve the tedium of long bus journeys. Before the fiftieth concert, I realised that I'd left some music in the previous town, and so, in the brief space between arrival and concert, Chris and Anne helped me to write out my part. We finished with minutes to spare – evident as crochets and quavers sped before me without their tails!

After Chris and Annette married, we shared a flat in Amsterdam for a few months. That year, I remember a dreary succession of white overcast skies, no sun, a sort of weather limbo. I left the orchestra and returned to London. Chris left a bit later and he and Annette went to Australia. They returned to London in 1966 and shared a house in Palmers Green with Sue and Frank Hawkins. Sue was an oboist and a great friend of Annette's. Simon was born that year, and Naomi the following year.

The life of a freelance musician is arduous, but Chris and Annette had a great circle of friends including many extraordinary musicians – one being Galina Solodchin, a White Russian brought up in Sydney and a student of Maurice Clare. She became leader of the Delme String Quartet. Until recently, she would fly to Australia each year to see her family, and always fitted in a flight to Melbourne to see Chris and Annette.

I am happy to recall that in 1980 when Chris attended the Indianapolis Violin Competition, he singled out Leonidas Kavakos as the outstanding talent despite the fact that first prize went to a Japanese violinist. Decades later, I totally share that early assessment by Chris as Leonidas Kavakos, now forty-four, is for me the outstanding violinist-musician of today.

A European tradition – Ronald Farren-Price AM

Ronald Farren-Price is a Principal Fellow of the Melbourne Conservatorium of Music, University of Melbourne, and has had a distinguished international career as a concert pianist. He is a former Dean of the Conservatorium and former Director of the Australian National Academy of Music.

The Melbourne Conservatorium of Music has an impressive history going back to the 1890s. I consider it a privilege to have been part of an institution that is the oldest and one of the largest music schools in Australia. Christopher Martin, I know, felt the same. He was here for twenty-six years and I have been here nearly twice as long, including some years as Dean.

Chris was appointed by Professor George Loughlin in 1972 and spent the most important part of his life here, when he was mature and vigorous. He had a particular role in this place: teaching violin and viola, conducting the orchestra and looking after chamber music. Being conductor of the orchestra meant that he reached all the instrumentalists bar the keyboard ones, though he did work with quite a number of pianists who played concertos.

Chris's contribution to the Con was quiet but of great depth. They don't come like that any more. There was a continuity with him, and students had that sense with the repertoire which they were being taught.

Chris, like myself, came from a rich heritage of European music, particularly that of the eighteenth, nineteenth and early twentieth century. We were the same age and inherited the same traditions. We weren't innovators in putting on the latest work that had just been written. From that point of view, Chris summed himself up very well when he said that he was a 'conservative conductor'.

In many ways, his was a golden time at the Con. There were quite a number of changes, though nothing as extensive as our current amalgamation with the Victorian College of the Arts. It means that we have a much bigger orchestra now, but there was something lovable about the orchestra that Chris used to direct.

One of Chris's great strengths was his knowledge of repertoire. Because of his association with orchestras in Europe and here, he was right in the thick of it. He also had a great knowledge of twentieth-century musicians. He was an important part of the chamber music scene in Melbourne as well, and was never happier than when he was playing such music. He loved it – just as he loved his conducting.

I've always found that the amount of music-making in England is fantastic, and Chris's own story is a remarkable example of that. I know he was conscious of not having passed his degree and would probably find it harder to get a job at the University today, but I have heard him say at meetings that if someone like RF-P came along and didn't get a job because he didn't have a Masters degree, it would be the most stupid thing in the world. Luckily, the University has given me an honorary doctorate!

Chris had to be taken for what he was and that was a very beautiful musician, very sensitive. He was not soloistic but his knowledge of music was profound, and he was an erudite speaker. His lecture every year to the postgraduate students on the violin as a physical instrument, for example, was always an important highlight.

Chris was a quiet persuader. He never did anything in a bombastic or fanfare way. He worked on the north side of the Con, in a room on the first floor – a lovely, big studio that was just right for him and suited him absolutely. He wasn't interested in the politics of the place or its administration. Such things didn't worry him. He would much prefer to take a class and study Beethoven's *Archduke Trio*. I think that's why he was so popular. He was very much loved by staff and students – particularly students.

Genesis of the Australian Doctors' Orchestra – Miklós (Miki) Pohl OAM

Miki Pohl is a consultant plastic and reconstructive surgeon practising in Melbourne. A very keen violinist and violist, he founded the Australian Doctors' Orchestra, which is celebrating its twentieth anniversary this year. He is also the founder of the European Doctors' Orchestra. He was honoured for services to Medicine and Music in 2002.

The first time I went to Chris's viola masterclass at the Mount Buller Chamber Music Summer School, I was very anxious. It takes a lot of courage to be exposed like that and I had heard that Chris could be a crotchety old bugger. I thought he would rip me to shreds. I was in my early forties and felt like a little boy as I played something for him. I told him that my playing and technique were stuck at a low level. After listening to me, he told me that my playing was rough and I was using the wrong part of the bow – but at the same time, he was very constructive. He suggested that I work away at certain Sevcik exercises and it really improved my playing.

Chris had a particular gift with amateurs. He could help them to find their best form. He had an easy manner, was knowledgeable, intensely musical and very likeable. He knew how far he could push us and that we were there principally because we loved playing and music. He went into a totally different mode with professionals and could be ruthlessly critical. Whenever I went to a concert with him, and it was always a concert of his own choosing, he would leave at the interval if it wasn't good. He'd had too many years of listening to really great music-making. If he didn't like what he was hearing and was unable to leave, he would lean forward, hold his head in his clenched hands and go to sleep. If it was good, he would be absorbed completely.

At the end of my first Music Camp at Mount Buller in 1993, I told Chris that I was forming the Australian Doctors' Orchestra and asked if he would conduct it. 'Yes, that'd be good', he said, and we immediately started working on the programme for our first concert later that year. There were seventy-four of us playing and about 250 people came to hear us in the Melba Hall. They loved it, we loved it, and we raised $4,000, which we gave to the Multiple Sclerosis Society. Chris chose this charity because of Jacqueline du Pré whom he knew well.

In the early years of the Doctors' Orchestra, we used to give one concert a year. As soon as the concert was over, we'd start programming the next one. Chris was brilliant at programming. It's a gift to know what will work and what won't with amateurs and with the constraints of rehearsal time. His other great gift was choosing soloists. Chris always put together the right people with the right programme. We've had the pleasure of working with great artists such as mezzo-soprano Suzannah Johnston, cellist Janis Laurs, violinist Carl Pini, violist Hartmut Lindemann and the fabulous violinist Elizabeth Wallfisch who is currently Professor of Baroque Violin at the Royal Academy of Music, London, and is director of the Wallfisch Band.

In our second concert, Carl Pini and Hartmut Lindemann played the Mozart's Sinfonia Concertante in E flat. I have never heard it played more beautifully. Another memorable concert was Sydney in 2002 with Elizabeth Wallfisch, Benjamin Martin and Niall Brown playing Beethoven's Triple Concerto. Chris chose Niall, who was the cellist with the Australian String Quartet at the time, because he was so comfortable playing in the high register needed for that work. Chris conducted the Australian Doctors' Orchestra for twelve years.

He would often come and stay with us when we lived in Tasmania. He became one of the family and a very good and trusted friend. One year, he suggested that I take my boys to the Riverina Summer Music Camp in Wagga. Initially I went with my oldest son Nick (cello), then gradually over the years all my four sons came – Will (violin), Carlie (viola) and Erik (double bass). It was always a wonderful week of music-making with the children in the presence of great artists.

Don Hazelwood, the renowned past concertmaster of the Sydney Symphony Orchestra (SSO), used to come. He and his daughter Jane, a violist with the SSO, and Jane's husband, Carl Pini, all came together. One year, Don sat at the back of the second violins behind a nine-year-old girl. When the music stopped, she turned and looked at him and said, 'Geez, you're good!' 'Thank you, my dear,' he replied. It was a beautiful moment.

Chris was well known for his commentary at the International Chamber Music Competition broadcast nationally by the ABC. He did it for many years – and I remember on one occasion actually being there at the Melba Hall hearing him talking about a young Israeli quartet. Chris loved them and said that the leader was the young Isaac Stern reincarnated.

Chris worked very hard at his music, though he wouldn't let on. He learned his scores inside out. Phillip Antippa told me that in performance Chris always had a score in front of him and sometimes would be conducting away, then stop and turn ten pages at once. He had an incredible memory.

My lessons with Chris were always based on the current programme we were preparing. I would have a concert coming up and would go to him with certain passages that I found difficult. If you're a professional, of course, you have all the exercises, scales and arpeggios at your fingertips. Amateurs, by and large, haven't. They reach a certain level then work away at pieces. Chris would talk about how to tackle a run, how to approach the fingering, how to capture the mood of the music and how to be well prepared when our section had an exposed part.

He was certainly most comfortable playing in quartets but he could play solo when he wanted to; after all, he was deputy lead in the Melbourne Symphony Orchestra at one time. I have seen videos of him playing the violin with his old friend Ron Davey, in Devon – virtuosic solo stuff – and all from memory. I also heard him at the age of eighty play Mozart's Synfonia Concertante with Spiros Rantos and the Chamber Strings of Melbourne. He had to sit to play but it was good, very good.

Chris had a very dark, broody side. I think that dogged him all his life. He was very self-critical and he never promoted himself. He used to say from time to time that he never conducted a professional orchestra, only amateur orchestras. While this may be true, he did conduct the orchestra at the Conservatorium and at music camps. He was very clear about what he wanted to do – that is, to present the works that he was at one with.

Chris did have difficulty when he retired from the Con aged sixty-six. His commentary on the ABC stopped at the same time and he was in limbo. He said, 'What am I going to do?' I suggested that he should do two things: join a Probus club and the University of the Third Age. He had never heard of either of them. Of course, he ended up conducting the U3A Orchestra and the numbers rose dramatically from nine players to sixty in no time at all and he worked with them for ten years. He went to Probus for a while, and he and I, Annette and Amanda Fairs played quartets for their Christmas party. That was fun. We'd play things like the music from *Fawlty Towers*, then we'd have dinner. Chris gave up his membership after two years. 'I can't stand it', he said. 'Too many old people.' Chris never felt old himself.

At his funeral, a member of the Conservatorium staff came to me with tears in his eyes and said, 'These days if you have no degree, do no research and don't publish, the University has no room for you'. More's the pity when you think what they are missing.

Real Musicians – Henry Wenig

Henry Wenig was associate principal cellist of the Melbourne Symphony Orchestra.

Chris and I saw each other often. We were long-term friends and loved to argue and discuss issues, although in reality we had similar tastes. He had played with the greatest, had heard the greatest and listened incessantly to all the luminaries of the classical music world. He prided himself on being of the Old School, but I suspect that he also saw himself as belonging to the Old World in his disdain for computers and above all in his hatred of the rampant commercialism and vulgarity of modern urban society. That is not to say that he was a musical snob. He would enthuse as sincerely about Bing Crosby or Frank Sinatra as he admired his beloved Jascha Heifetz.

His vast knowledge and experience remained regrettably overlooked and unused by the Melbourne music establishment. Perhaps it was because his attitudes differed from the trends he saw emerging there. In his own time, most musicians – even those who subsequently reached superstardom – were required to serve an apprenticeship, to undergo the slow climb up the ladder to musical maturity. He heartily disliked the cult of instant celebrity and was appalled by the attitude of a spokesman for the Yehudi Menuhin School who, when asked what happened to the graduates of the school, said that it was expected that they would all pursue a solo career and would never abase themselves by playing in an orchestra.

Although music was his passion and art his religion, Chris never lost a realistic perspective, knowing full well that musicians must eat, that music is a profession as well as an art. For him, music was above all a part of life. In his dealings with friends, colleagues and students, his charm, wit and humanity were always present. The audiences he addressed before or during the concerts he conducted loved his self-deprecating, unpretentious manner full of his own brand of whimsical English humour.

We had often played together as members of the MSO and in the Paul McDermott String Quartet. I saw a lot of him after he retired and in the years of the slow decline of his health. He knew full well that his days were numbered, but he accepted the situation with equanimity – without fuss or complaint. This proud Englishman gave a new and touching meaning to the concept of the British stiff upper lip. In his life and in his death, he was an example to us all and his passing away has left a big hole in my life.

All in good humour – John Curro AM, MBE

John Curro, violist, is one of Australia's most respected conductors, teachers and musicians. He is the director of the Queensland Youth Orchestras, which he founded in 1966. In 1976, he established the National Youth Concerto Competition, the most prestigious Australian competition for young string players. Previous winners include Richard Tognetti and Ray Chen.

Chris and I did about a dozen National Music Camps together. We all thought him a very gifted teacher, enthusiastic and inspiring. He loved tutoring at music camps and was perfect in that role, totally devoted to the students and supportive of young musicians. We had wonderful times playing chamber music together in the evenings.

There is a great tradition at music camp meals when a table composes a poem calling on one of the tutors to tell a joke. Campers hammer on the table tops until the staff member singled out complies. We all had to do it. If the students didn't like the joke, they would boo loudly. If they did like it, they would cheer. Chris always told fabulous jokes, often putting on perfect accents – Scots or Irish or whatever. He was certainly the most popular personality there.

We used to have a wonderful camp grace sung in rounds in three- or four-voice harmony: 'For life and health and daily food, we give you thanks, O Lord; for fellowship and all things good, we praise your name, O Lord'. It was stopped when the then CEO said that it might be offensive to non-Christians! It was a tradition of at least forty years.

Chris and I both bemoaned the fact that the people who ran the Australian Youth Orchestra didn't think that there were any conductors good enough in Australia, that they paid huge sums of money to bring in overseas people when often they could get someone as good and cheaper here.

Chris often came and stayed with me in Brisbane. We always played golf – he loved the game but was not a great player. I used to tell him to stop apologising and enjoy himself.

Chris was just as active in the music world in Australia as me – if not more so. We were like peas in a pod; we liked the same music, the same players and the same way of playing. He was a very sweet man, delightful and very sensitive.

Musical Circles – William Kimber

William Kimber is a general practitioner who studied piano with teachers from the Royal Academy of Music in London but opted for a medical career. His brother and sister are both distinguished violinists; Beryl is a Fellow of the Royal Academy of Music, Chris led the Boston Pops Orchestra before becoming Director of Strings at the Sydney Conservatorium.

The Kimbers and the Rosefields were prominent musical families in Melbourne. The three Rosefield girls were serious musicians, as were the three Kimber kids – me on the piano and my brother Chris and sister Beryl both on the violin. We had a lot to do with each other and all went to the National Music Camp at Geelong Grammar. It was a marvellous experience and we were incredibly enthusiastic. I had a friend, a clarinettist, who was tremendously proud to play the Beethoven C Major Concerto with Hephzibah Menuhin as the solo pianist. They had good conductors at the camp but you could tell that it was a youth orchestra. Now the students are so good, the standard is extraordinary. For the rest of the year after music camp, groups of us would play chamber music together in an ad hoc way. The Rosefield Trio was a prominent part of this.

In the 1950s, there was a lot of musical activity in Melbourne. The standard wasn't that high but it was pretty passionate. A lot of people were very married to their instruments and very fair dinkum about their commitment to music. And at that stage, if you really wanted to get anywhere you had to go overseas, usually to England or to the Juilliard School in America. My sister went to the Royal Academy of Music in London and my brother to the Guildhall School of Music and the Juilliard School. Gillian Rosefield went to study with Szymon Goldberg in Amsterdam and Annette studied with Tortelier in Paris.

I wouldn't call Australia a musical desert at that time. It was full of intensity but it needed polish from overseas. Apart from my own brother and sister and Gillian Rosefield, there were many fine Australian violinists who did well overseas – Paul McDermott was one, Brenton Langbein was another. Langbein formed an ensemble in Switzerland and came back one year to do a Musica Viva tour in Australia. Other musicians who went in the 1950s include Barry Tuckwell, the great horn player, who had a brilliant international career, and composer Malcolm Williamson, a Sydneysider, who eventually became Master of the Queen's Music.

When I came back to Melbourne in 1972, the general musical standard had risen appreciably. In the 1950s, the Melbourne Symphony Orchestra had a succession of rum old conductors but on my return, I found that both the conductors and the orchestra were of an international standard. In fact, the MSO was the first Australian orchestra to tour overseas.

There were a few chamber ensembles in Melbourne, of which the Paul McDermott String Quartet was perhaps the best established. They practised and performed to a high standard of professionalism. They weren't as brilliant as say the top international quartets like the Amadeus, but they were very good. Sydney had the Sydney String Quartet and the Australian String Quartet. Members of these quartets weren't completely dependent on their earnings as a quartet, because they were teachers and did individual solo work as well, but nonetheless they were established ensembles who got to know each other and played together for years.

I think I met Chris either through Paul McDermott or Annette, and throughout the 1970s and 1980s and into the 1990s we played regularly in ensembles of up to five players. We did practically all the piano quartets – Brahms' three piano quartets, Schumann, the Beethoven piano quartet written for wind but transcribed for strings and piano, the Mozart piano quartets – everything with the exception of Strauss, which I thought would be too hard for me. The core of our group was me and Chris and Annette, and we had a circle of violinists who would play with us, too.

We never got together just for a jam session. We played with a purpose, usually to perform at some place like Melba Hall at the Conservatorium, for suburban music societies or maybe at a private house in the country. We sometimes played piano quintets, including Brahms, Schumann, Dvořák and the Elgar Piano Quintet with Libby Hunt (Wallfisch).

Playing the Elgar was an opening experience for me, a growing experience. Elgar hadn't written much for the piano, so I had never played him. This was a major work and Chris captured the essence of its Englishness and brought it to our little music room rehearsals. Libby Hunt was, of course, a marvellous violinist. This was before she turned exclusively to the baroque. Elgar was romantic music at its best. The concert was for the English Speaking Music Society of Melbourne and we put a tremendous amount of work into it. It was held at St Peter's

Church Hall in Eastern Hill and I think we had an audience of five! It was a great tragedy and Libby nearly broke down in tears at the thought at the quality of the performance and the effort that had gone into it just for this little audience – and two of them were probably our relatives. We subsequently recorded the work for the ABC.

On another occasion, we played the Mozart Trio for Clarinet, Viola and Piano with Phillip Miechel, then principal clarinettist of the MSO. He was one of the greatest wind players they've ever had and he held that post for about thirty years.

Annette, Chris and I played a number of times for the Soirées Musicales either with Paul McDermott, Harry Hutchins, or my brother Chris. We also played for local music societies and in private houses, including Jascha Spivakovsky's place in St George's Terrace, by the river in Toorak – beautiful.

We would generally rehearse three or four times at my place in Armadale, because we had a music room and grand piano. We all loved the music that we were playing – a pretty traditional selection, the romantics, the classics, nothing much modern. Our programmes were made for a suburban rather than a sophisticated audience.

I learned a whole lot about music, about professionalism and interpretation and the various styles of different composers. Most of that came from Chris. I learned how to listen to the other players, how to stay cemented together, how to capture the mood of a work and how to listen to someone else's ideas even if they were different from your own. Chris knew every bit of chamber music repertoire; it was all in his head. He had played with some top-class pianists including Dohnányi and Nina Milkina, and he would often say, 'Well, Dohnányi did it this way'.

Rehearsals were very passionate but rarely unpleasant, though I remember a shouting match between Gillian Rosefield, Annette, Chris and Melville Cann, the second violin, over the Brahms Piano Quintet. I thought that it was going to end in blows, but it didn't. It was about the music – it wasn't personal. The level of communication at the Martins' home in Chrystobel Crescent was rarely below eight decibels. I was embarrassed until I realised that it was just their way. It was the same when the Rosefield women got together. There was always shouting. They were passionate people.

The first concert of the Doctors' Orchestra was a very happy event for me. Chris conducted and I played the Beethoven Third Piano Concerto in C Minor. It was a bit of a raggle-taggle ensemble, but Chris was used to amateur orchestras and knew how to keep them together and bring out the best in them. We had a guest horn player who had been with the MSO, as some of the music had significant horn parts and he was there to bolster it, but everybody else was a doctor. It was an enthusiastic performance and very well received. There was something on television about it. It was impressive how Chris developed that original group into the fine orchestra that it is now.

Chris had such a wide knowledge of the chamber music repertoire and interpretations that he was perfect for the ABC commentary doing the International Chamber Music Competition. He had a passion for quartets and understood the different ways of playing different composers, such as the Russian approach or the French approach. He knew the names of the people in the great quartets and usually had had some connection with them. It was all at his fingertips and he was confident and entertaining. After all, he had done it himself.

Viola players aren't ever well known among audiences, because they come well down on the programme after the leader, pianist and before the cellist. So Chris wasn't generally well known outside musical circles, but in musical circles everyone knew him and knew that he was an excellent and passionate musician, that he was extremely knowledgeable – including knowledge on the subject of violins and bows.

Annette had a beautiful bow which she lent to my son Tom, a cellist. He had it in his room lying across the chair and inadvertently sat on it one day just before Chris and Annette were due to arrive for a rehearsal. Bows can be repaired but they are never the same, they never regain the same kind of bounce. I couldn't look at Annette when they arrived and the first thing she said was, 'I've left my bow behind. You can give me the one that Tom's using.' I had to say, 'He sat on it. It's broken.' I felt horrible.

At that stage, I had a lot of Greek patients who paid in cash – this was before Medicare – and I presented Annette with a bagful of money saying, 'Take this'. All she could say was, 'Oh Joe, Joe!' (my family nickname). They got it repaired. It was beautifully done and you couldn't see where the break had been, and people who have played with it said that it was fine, but even so it was an agony. Tom still gets a knot in his stomach every time he thinks of it.

Although I did not see so much of Chris in later years, I did see him before he died and the old intimacy of playing together was still there. Making music with other people creates a special bond; you have to give some, take some, try and contribute. You don't want to be the doormat who fits in with everybody. You want to express your part, but at the same time listen to the others all the time and work with them. In that sense, Chris and Annette were ideal rehearsal mates.

Corpus Medicorum – Phillip Antippa

Phillip Antippa is a cardiothoracic surgeon based at the Royal Melbourne Hospital, where he is director of the Lung Cancer Service. He is also a member of the Lung Cancer Service team at the Peter MacCallum Hospital. He founded Corpus Medicorum in 2002 and is a founding member of the Australian Doctors' Orchestra.

If I had to write an epithet for Chris, I would have to say that he was the finest and the most underrated musician I have ever known and that his talents were completely unexploited. He really, really was the most musical person. You could see it; you could hear it. When he raised his baton, you'd know that it would work.

I started playing the piano at five years of age and the violin at eight, and I switched to the viola when I was about eleven or twelve because they needed one for the senior orchestra. I was at Carey Grammar School where there was a reasonably strong music programme. The violin teacher was fine, but not particularly strong, so switching to the viola at fifteen meant that I had to get another teacher and my mother found Chris.

I remember turning up at the house in Chrystobel Crescent where Annette still lives. I was taught in a dark room with a big piano and lots of sheet music and heavy rugs. Chris was inspiring and we formed a strong bond. We would often spend half an hour just talking and looking at different things. Chris would put up a piece of music and I'd play. He'd say, 'Well, you can play it', and he'd drive through line by line and just change it with his finger. Chris was not really heavy on technique and even if I hadn't practised much we would find interesting things to do. I only realised later how much of his musicality rubbed off on me during those times.

When I went to Melbourne University, I had a bursary with Chris at the Conservatorium. I was in a position where I could have chosen music. Many of us were, and we thought: do we study hard and become a musician and head off into the great unknown or do we do the safe thing and become surgeons? The latter is a much, much easier road and your job's guaranteed. To be a professional musician is very hard. Either you're one of the best or you're regarded as mediocre. I think Chris felt that unless I knew I was going to be really great, I wouldn't have pushed on in music. Had he said to me, 'Phillip, you're a really fantastic musician, you should consider a career in music', I would have. But he never did.

Not that he was unkind – certainly not – but he was not forthcoming with praise about anything. A compliment from Chris was rare. I think I only heard him say a couple of times, 'That's a good solo, you played it well'. He would be encouraging and say, 'Yes, that's fine', but that's not the same thing.

Chris was involved with music camps for many years and I think that's how he honed his conducting skills. He regretted that he had never been offered the chance to conduct a professional orchestra. There's a good history of that lack of recognition in this country. I've played in a lot of orchestras now and Chris would still be the best conductor I've ever played with.

A lot of people who are involved with music don't understand the importance of a conductor. 'Conductors just stand up there waving their hands around', they say. It's hard to put into words exactly how a conductor works and what a great sound a good conductor can produce. When Chris was the conductor and he had things his way – and his way was not always to everyone's taste – he was certainly extraordinary.

I was recently in England and played with the European Doctors' Orchestra. It's a great little orchestra, Corpus Medicorum level, fabulous players, but the conductor is a surgeon and an amateur and that was by far and away the weakest point of the whole orchestra. If you're going to pay anyone to stand in front of you, the conductor is absolutely crucial. I think that the success of Corpus Medicorum and the reason it's kept going was entirely because of Chris.

As his student, I'd play a piece *à la* Chris Martin and that was how it worked, without any intellectualisation. I hesitate to use the word 'intuitive' as I don't think it's a compliment. It's almost a derogatory word, because it implies that you know what you want to do but you can't explain what you're doing. For a scientist, I think that's bad. There's always an explanation for it, just that we can't put it into words. In music, what it really means is experience, taste and knowledge – knowing what works and what doesn't work. And that describes Chris. And not just his conducting, but also the way he chose programmes. He always chose fabulous programmes for our orchestra. He knew exactly what would work, what the crowd would like, and what was easy to rehearse given our strengths and weaknesses.

Also because of Chris's music camp experience, he was extraordinarily good with amateurs. To be able to conduct amateurs well is even more difficult than conducting professionals, because they're harder to rehearse, you don't always get what you want and they're not always there. This made Chris a perfect fit for the Doctors' Orchestra, which I joined when Miki formed it in 1992.

Corpus Medicorum was born as a small string orchestra in Melbourne in 2002, doing three concerts a year at Melba Hall. We kept that same model as the Doctors' Orchestra and helped to raise money for the hospital. We gradually grew to a chamber orchestra, had a small wind section and started doing bigger works and other things. Then we outgrew Melba Hall, both from an ensemble size and an audience size, and moved to the Iwaki Auditorium. Acoustically it's amazing and there's plenty of room for the orchestra, though for the audience it's a bit like watching a basketball game. It's not really designed to be an auditorium.

Chris's contribution to the Corpus Medicorum was consummate. It was integral. Without him, it wouldn't have happened. To get amateurs to play things well, you need to have a high level of professionalism in certain areas – first and foremost in conducting, then in overall musicianship and in programme direction – otherwise amateur performers flounder.

Chris was proud of the orchestra, he enjoyed it and thought that it was good. I always made sure that we did the best for him. That's how you played for Chris. Regarding the programme, I'd always ask about things and he'd respond, 'Don't be ridiculous' or 'You can do this'. There were things that he knew we could play that he wouldn't do because they were so special to him, such as the Vaughan Williams *Tallis*, one of his favourite pieces, or Elgar's *Sospiri*. When he finally included these beautiful English pieces in a programme, Chris was too sick to conduct the concert himself and Keith Crellin did it.

Chris's last concert in December 2010 was the standout for me. We did Beethoven No. Six, a work that I played in my youth. Chris had a way with Beethoven that was extraordinary. Although he loved his English music, his Beethoven was really very, very fine. He understood it and knew it; he knew what we wanted out of it and it worked. He always said that we were a Beethoven orchestra, which was one of those very rare compliments from Chris. At the end of the concert, he was unwell. We pushed him and he pushed himself. That concert just about killed him – maybe that's why it was so memorable. He was fantastic.

A lovely conductor – Rowan Thomas

Rowan Thomas is deputy director of Anaesthesia at St Vincent's Health, Melbourne. He is president of the Doctors' Orchestra and was concertmaster for eighteen years. He is also a founding member of Corpus Medicorum.

Chris wanted to be true to the beauty and perfection in everything that he had anything to do with, not only with his own music but with anyone he was teaching. I switched from viola to violin when I was twenty and the first pieces I learned were *Zigeunerweisen* by Sarasate and the violin concerto by Mendelssohn. This was really jumping in the deep end and my teacher, Barbara Argall, was becoming frustrated that I couldn't get on top of the Mendelssohn. I had studied viola with Chris some years before and went to see him for some tips, some pointers. I played him the Mendelssohn. He listened and said, 'You know what? I must have heard hundreds of people play this, thousands of times, over thirty years. I've never heard it played well and today is no exception. Why don't you just put it away and pick it up again when you're forty? You'll understand it better then.'

When you're studying music, you have to be able to embrace pretty stringent comments. If people are gentle around the edges and don't tell you what they think, you never actually get the true message and don't move forward. What Chris was saying was that there were too many things I needed to build on and create in my technique and my understanding of the music to be able to make the enormous leap to playing it well at that point. I think he was right.

I used to be in Chris's orchestra at music camp. He was a lovely conductor. You don't realise when you're young the skill involved. Rehearsals were relaxed and fun and he'd tell a bundle of jokes in different accents, but on the night he'd work it up. He knew people were nervous and would really be paying attention and he would communicate something extra. Looking back, I understand better what he imparted with his hands, what he did with the beat and with the music.

There were three orchestras at camp. I don't know why Chris was never the first orchestra conductor. I think it was the small poppy thing. He was here and the first orchestra conductor was often someone from overseas. For the second orchestra, when I was at camp, it was either John Curro or Chris Martin, both very professional, extremely competent and artistic – as good as any in Australia – and the third was usually an up-and-coming conductor who needed the experience and exposure.

Music camp underwrote the social value of music for me. It brought together all sorts of people from different backgrounds – people you may or may not like or be able to talk to, with whom you sat down and played music. There was always a step up in ability and lasting friendships. A lot of the professional musicians around Australia today, like Bill Hennessy and Eric Clay, were at music camp with me.

I learned viola at school, then privately with Barbara Argall, and when I got to seventh grade and more complex pieces, she said, 'These are getting too hard, you need to go to someone like Chris Martin'. So I went to Chris for lessons in Hawthorn for about a year before he went on sabbatical. I was about sixteen or seventeen. He exposed me to the entire viola repertoire very, very quickly as we worked on pieces, not scales or studies. Eventually he said to me, 'You're good, but it's not right. There's talent all over the place but it needs to be contained. It needs to be put into a box. I'm not sure that I'm the right person to trap it, control it and put it in the box. You need someone who will do that. It may be Spiros Rantos. He's very disciplined and a prime player. He's coming to Melbourne – you can learn from him.' So I did.

Spiros actually lived in Chris's house while he and the family went to England for a year and I found him the complete opposite as a teacher.

He thought that the pieces I was playing were too hard, and he talked about rhythm and the weight of the beat in the bar, explaining that the heaviest beat is the first, the next heaviest is the third, then the second and fourth. It was like rocking backwards and forwards, backwards and forwards. He would also listen to me playing scales for an hour. Chris was right – it did suit me better.

I became involved in the Australian Doctors' Orchestra right at the start. I was at the Mount Buller Chamber Music Summer School in 1993 and playing with my quartet on the first day when this guy came over and watched intently every single note I played. I was a bit unnerved. It turned out to be Miki Pohl. He said to me, 'I'm thinking of starting a doctors' orchestra and I think I've found the leader. You'll be concertmaster and I'll organise it. Do you think we can do it?'

Miki had a list of musical doctors and got his secretary to contact them. There were more than seventy for the first concert. It's grown to around 160 players, which is huge. The full Melbourne Symphony Orchestra is eighty. The 160 would frighten some conductors, but Chris managed well. He did have some special requests. He wanted the front two desks of all the strings to be really strong, good players so that he could actually connect with them. He also wanted stronger players towards the back, which is the opposite to how people would normally sit. It's important because strong players at the back keep the beat, support the whole orchestra and hold everything together, thus avoiding what Chris called the 'Mantovani effect' – a ripple of different rhythms through the orchestra.

A lot of what Chris did as a conductor was to communicate with his movements rather than words, though I do remember one occasion when the first violins were doing something that he wasn't happy with and he said, 'That was terrible, first violins! Can you start off with a little more confidence and make the third "E" the actual point of the phrase? Your "F" naturals were out of tune, while the rest has to be a little more shaped, and then a flourish as it comes down will give it a bit of a positive note, a swing. Right? Let's give it a go.' We played it through and he was stunned. 'My God, you actually did all that!', he said.

A concertmaster is meant to be the nexus between the conductor and orchestra. Often the conductor is a pianist or wind player and doesn't understand string technique, so the concertmaster translates what is required. We also decide what is a down bow or an up bow. If the orchestra is lost, it's the concertmaster who guides it back. Chris would sometimes tease me a bit and say, 'Rowan, you're doing what everybody else was doing. I want you to do what I'm doing. You're meant to be with me.' In other words, I don't care if I'm wrong, you've got to be wrong with me.

Chris and Annette and Miki and I would sometimes play quartets together. One night Miki said, 'Let's play Brahms'. 'When will amateurs understand you cannot sight-read Brahms!' exclaimed Chris. Certainly for the first violin parts, when you're sight-reading something, it's like riding a motorcycle really, really fast on the Great Ocean Road. Somehow you're hanging on and zooming into corners and skidding around. I'm always amazed that my fingers can move. There's something about the body that makes it all work and you hang in there for dear life. How it happens, I have no idea. It's just one of those little mysteries.

Closer to home (1) – Simon Martin

Simon Martin is the eldest of Chris and Annette Martin's children. He is a rhythm and blues guitarist.

He clears his throat and, with soft voice and deft timing, he calls attention around the room. Hunched forward slightly and cupping his soft hands as if telling the story for the first time. Older now but still handsome, with his striking features – the gap in his front teeth, his steel wool hair – and gentle voice permeating through my family life up until the present.

Without this person, my world will be a darker and harsher place. His passing has brought me indescribable sadness. He always showed those in his presence the gentlest side of humanity. He was dignified, intelligent, extremely musical and artistic, but most of all he was the gentlest person I knew and I was absolutely proud to be able to refer to him as 'Dad'.

Closer to home (2) – Benjamin Martin

Benjamin Martin is a pianist and composer. A graduate of the Juilliard School, he was conducted frequently by his father as a soloist with the Doctors' Orchestra, Corpus Medicorum and the Chamber Strings of Melbourne. He has appeared regularly with the Australian Chamber Orchestra and the Firebird Trio. His compositions have been performed in Europe and the United States.

It is often said about artists that to know them by their art is enough; how they choose to live is unimportant. Dad believed this strongly, and yet I feel that there was much to appreciate about him that extended beyond his artistry. For the purposes of this book, I would like to share a little of what I knew of him as a musician.

There was much – so much – that he did during his life without making a song and dance about it, partly out of modesty, partly out of a perfectionism that convinced him his own efforts were never up to scratch. As a result, he remained *con sordino* about many of his own heartfelt musical offerings.

Dad has described his early life in his 'Memoir', but what he didn't mention was the coincidence that the house in which we grew up in Chrystobel Crescent, Hawthorn, and where Mum still lives, used to belong to the great cellist, Lauri Kennedy. Lauri was the father of cellist John Kennedy, with whom Dad played in the London String Quartet in the 1960s, and grandfather of violinist Nigel Kennedy. Small world.

I fear that Dad would already be shuffling his feet at all this detail, much preferring a good joke. Unfortunately I am a poor joke-teller, whereas Chris was one of the best. His many visits to National Music Camp as a conductor earned him the reputation as a wonderful musician with a charming, cavalier wit. Another Music Camp conductor, the extraordinary musician Georg Tintner, once complimented my father profusely after one of his performances, something Georg hardly ever did. Such praise from a fellow perfectionist meant a great deal to Dad. He would also be thrilled to know that Elizabeth Wallfisch will be naming after him the chamber orchestra that she is to conduct at the National Music Camp in 2013.

Dad once said to me that art sorts people out. I don't think he meant that art was the supreme arbiter – he was never an 'art is my religion' kind of person – but simply that, for better or worse, we inevitably reveal ourselves through art.

Dad loved good quotations, and one he liked and which I think applied to him is this by Thomas Aquinas: 'It is greater to be worthy of honour than to be honoured'. Dad was a difficult man to honour in the normal fashion. A group of friends wanted to nominate him for an AM but, being content with his solitary British passport, he proved ineligible. Anyone who knew him was never in any doubt that his acute sensibilities, sharp sense of humour and modest nature were above all English. He read *Pride and Prejudice* no fewer than sixteen times. Even his love of wildlife was above all English. His beloved *Birds of Britain* accompanied him on his forest walks in Devon and Cambridge (where he spent his sabbatical in 1977) and remained on the shelf when he moved to Melbourne.

His love of art and nature were probably one and the same thing, and it's no accident that Dad's favourite Beethoven symphony was the *Pastoral* – a work which he conducted beautifully with Corpus Medicorum for his last concert, just over a year before he died. In fact, in the days before his death, Dad was reading *Penguin Island* by Anatole France, given to him by his friend Herbert Baer. He was captivated by France's description of how the penguins recoiled from their neighbours, the porpoises, simply because they were neighbours. 'Just as it is in the world', he said.

Dad was also a man of ritual. From an early age, we three children were accustomed to the morning sounds of a teaspoon tinkling against the inside of one, two, then three cups of tea, followed by the obligatory three taps on each rim. Then there was the warm-up that he performed whenever he picked up his violin: a few bars of Elgar's Violin Concerto and some of Saint-Saëns' *Havanaise*. I can still go through the entire warm-up in my mind, each excerpt seamlessly and beautifully interwoven. Then the bell would ring and someone would arrive – perhaps with a violin to sell – and then we'd hear the warm-up once again.

As Mum often said, Dad had an amazing talent as a string player. When he was eighty, he performed Mozart's *Duo Concertante* with Spiros Rantos and the Chamber Strings with extraordinary grace. He'd hardly touched his viola for decades before picking it up for a few weeks before going onstage at the concert. This is not to say that he didn't suffer from performance nerves, as his story about *Harold in Italy* with the Melbourne Symphony Orchestra at the Myer Music Bowl in 1983 illustrates.

He walked out in front of 10,000 people and performed the opening marvellously, but then great gusts of wind shot through the stage, blowing stands and music all over the place. Dad stood for a while along with the other bewildered members of the orchestra before leaving the stage. It was really quite biblical. The following day, he read a review which stated that he hadn't projected enough!

Dad never called himself a religious man but he was nonetheless a deeply spiritual person and in his final days was greatly moved by Janet Baker's singing of Mahler's *Urlicht* (*Primal Light*) from the Resurrection Symphony. The song is a wish to be released from worldly miseries, to discover freedom from this life. The night Dad died, I thought to myself that a gentle soul has passed through the gates.

Closer to home (3) – Naomi Martin

Naomi Martin is Christopher Martin's middle child and the only girl. She studied violin with Nathan Gutman and then the viola, having some lessons from her Dad. She attended several music camps and got into the Melbourne Conservatorium by the skin of her teeth, however chose to study Chinese medicine and healing instead. She continued to play in amateur orchestras and music camps and occasionally picks up the violin or viola to play a tune.

In about 2004, I spent six months in England as I wanted to connect with Dad's family. I had some lovely times with my Aunt Betty, his sister. She lived in the tiniest house in Somerset, with not much more than one room. I got lost on the way and she actually walked to where I was. I realised afterwards that it must have been hard for her as she didn't walk much at all. I was glad to be able to spend time with her. She was lonely and beginning to get confused, but I liked her. She was good company.

Betty and I went together to put flowers on her husband's grave in the churchyard, and while I was with her in Somerset I got more of a sense of where Dad comes from. She was very west country, very parochial. She was also a little bit unpredictable and I don't think that she and Dad were close when they were young. I believe that she was more her father's daughter, but when she and Dad were together you could see that the two of them understood each other very well, though she had a lot more of the country in her than he did.

I also saw Betty's son, Phillip, and his wife and three children. He's my only cousin on Dad's side, so really my trip was more about my connecting with the country than with Dad's family because there were so few of them. I think that it was beyond Betty to imagine Dad's life as being so different, but I know that his Mum was very proud.

I don't remember my grandfather at all. I only met him once when I was a baby and later heard that he had been traumatised by the war. I do remember staying in Tiverton with my grandmother, when I was nine, and being utterly present as she was talking. Mum has a photograph of the three of us children with our heads up, listening as Granny's telling us this story, and we were completely there with her.

My brothers and I grew up in an amazing environment with music happening all the time. In bed at night, I could always hear Mum and Dad tuning up and practising. They played in a quartet and I loved going to sleep listening to them play. I got to learn many pieces of music that way, some of which I never knew the names for. I took the music for granted, and when I stayed with friends I missed it.

Other people's houses seemed so quiet in comparison to ours, however well they got along. Our family didn't always get along. It was noisy and chaotic but there was always humour. Dad told new jokes every day. We had many, many years of new jokes. I don't know where he got them from but he told them very well, usually at meal times. Every one of us has a strong sense of humour – and that's such a saving grace.

I played second violin in the Chamber Strings of Melbourne and rehearsals were always fun. Dad was moody sometimes but with good reason. He would tell stories and jokes and have everyone relaxed and happy, and then he might get stressed because a piece of music was not together and it was time to work. Getting that balance right was hard for him; the jokey side, 'I am everybody's equal', against the serious side, 'now I have to play conductor and be in charge'. Even in our family, I think there was always that tension.

When I was seventeen, the Chamber Strings did a tour to England. We travelled around on a bus and poor Miss Cameron was forever telling us off and she'd be telling Dad off, too, in the same breath. That tour included a concert in Tiverton and Dad and I stayed with Granny. I was very distracted at the time but I do remember reading Dad's diary and finding it fascinating. I don't know how old he was when he wrote it, but

Granny had kept it. It was very earnest. While we were there, I met Ron Davey who was a real character and had a pet parrot.

In Tiverton, Dad showed me places that were special to him as a boy, like the bridge over the river, made of big flat stones. Those times were very intimate. I found a picture of this bridge in his flat the other day and it took me right back there. Dad was very relaxed about being in Tiverton; it was just as if he was popping back home. The hard part was leaving his Mum.

I was never tempted to become a musician. I remember once writing in my Year 8 autobiography that I really wanted to be a writer but that, if I was really desperate, I could always be a musician. I only had the occasional music lessons with Dad, but I remember once trying to learn a piece from music camp. It was really hard and I was going out of my mind with it and went out into the back yard tearing my hair out. Dad followed me and said, 'Come on, come on'. He took me through the music and, amazingly, within about ten minutes I had it. It was a question of getting the rhythm. He was a very good teacher like that – very patient, very clear, very comforting.

Closer to home (4) – Emma Martin

Emma Martin, Simon's daughter, was born in 1993 and until Naomi's daughter, Edith, was born in 2010, she was Chris's only grandchild. Emma gave the following eulogy at Chris's funeral on behalf of both of them.

I thought I was prepared, as you get to a stage where you think that it'll happen any day now. But when it happens, I'm not ready. I know my grandpa meant a great deal to a lot of people. It's a bit strange for me to think of so many people knowing my grandfather in a musical way. I knew him in a grandpa way – the family side of him. To me, he was the really gentle, kind-hearted, generous, loving man who loved all things French and British. He was there for me since I learned to talk and walk. He would read to me when I was little, buy me a whole roll of film so that when I stayed over I could take pictures all day, and at family dinners he would make a special effort to take anything out of the food that I didn't like or compensate with a whole other dish. In classic grandpa style, when asked for change by a homeless guy, he replied, 'Sorry, I've only got hundreds', went home and came back with $10.

Grandpa helped to look after me since I was born. Every Saturday morning until I was about six, he would pick me up from my grandma's and take me to the Maranoa Gardens in Balwyn. Getting back in the car could be a problem sometimes, running around the car and making the seventy-year-old man chase me. I never really thought of him as the grandpa who taught music and was so involved in that. My grandpa would go out in search of the biggest turkey on the farm at Christmas, talk about the boring green vegetables and how much he hated them, and share stories that captivated the round table.

Some people never get the chance to be close to their grandparents, but I got that chance. I got an extra ten years with grandpa. As he got older, he began to appreciate the little things in life and I began to appreciate him more – like within two days of moving to the hospice, he fell in love with a gum tree that, at the right time, he said had a 'magnificent light'.

He used to talk to me about the war when he asked what I was studying at school. It's only now that I wish I had asked for more stories to remember him by. I was fascinated to hear how he got to throw grenades and fire a tank and was proud of him, in a way.

A few months before he died, I asked him if there was anything he would like to give me that really meant something to him. He thought about it and about a week later came back with a really old wallet. It was his father's during the war. When the fighting was over, everyone was given twenty sovereigns. The first thing his father did was to go and buy his mum a wedding ring, which left him with half a sovereign. He kept this in the wallet and never spent it. The wallet never meant as much to me as it does now.

Between conductors – John Hopkins OBE

John Hopkins was born in Yorkshire in 1927 and held a number of conducting positions in Britain before going to New Zealand at the age of thirty to conduct the National Orchestra of the New Zealand Broadcasting Service and the New Zealand Opera Company. He came to Australia in 1963, when he took up the position of director of Music for the ABC. He is currently Emeritus Professor of Conducting at the University of Melbourne.

Iris Rosefield invited me to stay at their home in 1963 while I was in Melbourne to conduct a series of summer concerts in Melbourne and, while I was there, her daughter Annette arrived from England with her husband, Christopher Martin. Chris and I played chamber music together with Frank Pam and Jo Beaumont. I enjoyed his wry sense of humour and his wonderful stories. He seemed very English.

Both Chris and Annette played with the Melbourne Symphony Orchestra. It was considered second to the Sydney Symphony Orchestra then, the poor relation. It was slightly smaller than the SSO but had a history of good players, especially in the wind section with Dick Chubb, Gabor Reeves, the principal clarinettist, Jiri Tancibudek, principal oboc, and Tom Wightman, a bassoonist from the London Symphony Orchestra. They were star players. In 1964 John Bishop, Professor of Music at the University of Adelaide, invited Reeves, Tancibudek and Wightman to form the University of Adelaide Wind Quintet. This was devastating to the MSO, which already had a difficult situation with the conductor Georges Tzipine. He was a likeable man, but not an experienced enough conductor of the symphony repertoire to command the whole-hearted support of the fine players in the orchestra.

There was a lot of music for young people in Melbourne in the 1960s, owing to the work of Dr Alexandra Cameron in the schools and to John Bishop and Ruth Alexander who founded the Music Camp movement. The first National Music Camp was held at Point Lonsdale in 1947. I went to the one held at Geelong Grammar in 1963 and stayed with the Rosefields. Jo Beaumont led the first orchestra. The camps were not as strong then as they are now, because of their small budgets, but there was lots of enthusiasm. I have since been to many music camps which Chris also attended. He was happy to work at any level.

Chris did remarkable things for music in Melbourne. His great love for English music was important and came out in his performances. He was the ideal person to conduct the Chamber Strings of Melbourne. Some of the players were not full-time music students and he handled them beautifully. The orchestra has been so successful because of his musicianship and personality and Dr Cameron's determination. One of the loveliest experiences I ever had was conducting the Chamber Strings at St John's Church in Southbank, with Chris Martin and Spiros Rantos playing the Mozart Symphonia Concertante, when Chris was nearly eighty.

Chris was a most generous, warm person, a delight to spend time with. As well as the his work with the Chamber Strings of Melbourne, his work with the Australian Doctors' Orchestra was outstanding. I have heard some marvellous performances that he gave with them. He always went for the heart of the music.

Contributing on all levels – Kerry Murphy

Kerry Murphy is Professor of Music and Head of Musicology at the Melbourne Conservatorium of Music at the University of Melbourne. She is a founding member of the UK Arts and Humanities Research Council Network Francophone Music Criticism 1789–1914, and since 2006 has been an Honorary Associate (and Australian corresponding member) of the Centre for the History of Music in Britain, the Empire and the Commonwealth in the UK. She was a member of the artistic advisory board of the Victorian Opera Company from 2007 to 2011.

Christopher Martin was a compassionate, humble, incredibly erudite man with a keen sense of the ridiculous and a fine wit. He was one of the most musical people I have ever encountered and someone capable of inspiring a love of music in all who came under his spell. I would defy anyone to know as much as Chris about violins – yet he wore his knowledge so lightly. He also saw through hypocrisy and pretension. He himself was straight and honest.

Perhaps Chris's greatest contribution here at the Conservatorium was the string players whom he developed. He was not only a fabulous teacher, he had an encyclopaedic knowledgeable of instruments and bows. One of the first things people did when they were planning to buy a violin was to take it to Chris and see what he thought. He might pick it up, look at it and say, 'No, it's not worth it', or 'Yes, this is a fine instrument'. He could have been a dealer. He had the same skills with bows. Other people would charge for this sort of knowledge, but Chris wouldn't have dreamed of it. I used to get him to come and talk to my postgraduate students on violins and, in particular, on bows. There wasn't anyone in Australia with such knowledge.

One of Chris's great achievements was to persuade Dorcas McClean to leave her violin to the Con to be sold in order to set up the Dorcas McClean Travelling Scholarship for Violinists. It is one of the biggest violin scholarships in Australia. Dorcas McClean was a very gifted player, the leader of the Melbourne Symphony Orchestra, and Chris knew that she had this incredible instrument. She died in 1981.

There were people on the staff who really appreciated Chris, including the librarians Margaret Greene and Christine Webster. Margaret and Christine both had a good sense of humour and thoroughly enjoyed Chris Martin, and the respect was mutual. For much of Chris's time at the Con, there was also a tea lady called Elsie with whom he got on extremely well. Chris was not a political being and did not put himself forward; he treated everyone as equal.

When a first-year University student, I stopped my main instrument, the piano, but wanted to continue violin in order to play in orchestras. I had violin lessons with Chris at Chrystobel Crescent and would approach the house dragging my feet, because I hadn't practised – again! Chris told me years later that he used to watch me and say to himself, 'Ah, here comes that girl who never does any practice'. But I used to learn so much, because I encouraged Chris to talk to distract him from my lack of practice. He would tell me about past musicians and play selections from his music collection. He had an extraordinary recording of Heifetz's variations on *Carmen*.

I often used to go and listen to Chris and Annette playing chamber music at the Caulfield Branch of the Victorian Music Society and at the Soirées Musicales in Coppin Hall. I went with my mother and have never forgotten some of those concerts. They were mainly Schumann and Schubert – the romantic repertoire. There were many Jewish people in the audience who knew the music well and loved it. That was one of the attractions – being part of an audience that was so knowledgeable. Those concerts were a vivid part of my adolescence.

I had lessons with Chris for a number of years and always felt that I was one of his worst students. When I was seventeen or eighteen, I played in the Melbourne Baroque Ensemble which he conducted. He had so many students then that he could never remember my name, and he used to call out, 'Hey you, up the back of the seconds!'

Chris related emotionally to the music and could convey this sense of emotional connection to people learning from him either individually or in a group. He was also one of the funniest people I have ever met and every minute of orchestra was fun. He had so many anecdotes – I particularly remember the Beecham stories and incredible jokes. He could go on for hours.

Today you'd expect a group called the Baroque Ensemble to pay some attention to playing in the baroque style, but Chris was as romantic as anything. He adored baroque music but we all played with full vibrato. Chris's later success with the Chamber Strings of Melbourne was incredible. Above all, he loved conducting English music. It was part of his soul.

Ham and Eggs – Edwina Kayser

Edwina Kayser is a freelance violinist and teacher who studied at the University of Melbourne and the Guildhall School of Music and Drama in London. She has worked with orchestras in the UK, Portugal and Australia. As well as teaching at Trinity Grammar School and Westbourne Grammar School, she plays with Orchestra Victoria and is a member of the highly successful Aequales Ensemble.

I was sixteen when I joined the Chamber Strings of Melbourne. There were about twenty-four of us. My desk partner was called Sam and from the start we were 'Ham and Eggs'. This was typical of Chris; he had a real warmth and rapport with students. I was 'Eggsie' for years. Musically, Chris had a great feel for the shape and direction of a phrase. He never talked about playing louder or softer, faster or slower but always in terms of images or stories. It would make us play in a much more personal way. For example, with the opening of the Elgar Serenade for Strings he told us to imagine newborn lambs, unsteady on their feet, gradually gaining confidence. He would compare a musical figure to leaves floating to the ground and the start of a note being like warm air blown on glass.

There was nothing wishy-washy about Chris. He wouldn't tolerate sloppy playing and could get quite angry at times and once threw the baton. We always got into trouble if we did an unmusical fingering. He was very particular about the sound.

Chris had beautiful hands as a conductor. I never felt that he just beat time, rather he took us on a journey. Often he would let the orchestra play and would sit and listen, letting us take over what he had set up. He didn't feel that he had to control everything. It's very empowering as a musician to be given all that direction in rehearsal and be allowed to own it. The music that we played was quite demanding but Chris was careful to choose works the orchestra could manage. That meant everything we played was played really well. The standard was very high.

I went on my first tour with the Chamber Strings in 1985. It was fantastic. We went to Chris's home town of Tiverton, where Chris played the Telemann Viola Concerto with the orchestra, his daughter Naomi in the violin section and his mum sitting in the front row – so proud. It was very emotional.

As a student at the Conservatorium, I studied with Chris for a year before changing to Carl Pini – at Chris's insistence. He felt that Carl was the better teacher. We didn't have a chamber music component as part of the course, but Chris put me into a string quartet and he tutored us every week for a couple of hours. He introduced us to so much repertoire and guided us in the works we chose ourselves. He knew every quartet part from memory and would play them all on his viola, demonstrating the point he wanted to make. He had a phenomenal memory for music. He taught us to listen to the other parts and be constantly aware of the function of our own part.

I think there's a sense that chamber music in Melbourne only really started with the International Festival that Marco van Pagee set up and the huge growth of chamber music that has come out of that. It's undeniably true that it has had a huge impact, but there was quite a healthy scene before that. While at the Con, for example, there wasn't an official chamber music subject. Chris facilitated something like that to happen.

Both at the Con and with Chamber Strings, Chris constantly told us about his personal experiences with composers and musicians. When he played Benjamin Britten, for example, he would say that we had to do the bowing in a particular way because that's how Britten did it.

Chris invited me to play the Bach Double Violin Concerto (or the 'Dark Bubble', as he called it) and Vaughan Williams' *Lark Ascending* with the U3A Orchestra. It was an honour to play the Bach with Chris because of his wonderful sound and phrasing. Everyone in that orchestra loved playing for Chris. He could coax a beautiful sound from them and never made the players feel that they weren't good enough. He was also a tremendously popular conductor with the Stonnington Symphony. When Chris conducted, there were fourteen desks of violas – practically stretching out the door!

The last concert I played with him was for Corpus Medicorum, to celebrate his eightieth birthday. He chose to end the programme with a very English work – Elgar's *Introduction and Allegro*. On stage were musicians and friends of all ages, from a past Sydney Symphony Orchestra concertmaster and current Melbourne Symphony Orchestra concertmaster to medical professionals, students from Chamber Strings of Melbourne and of course many of his former pupils. There wasn't a dry eye on stage, and Chris chose to end it by reading a charming and witty letter from *The Times* newspaper about when a cuckoo coos in the major key!

Chris had an incredible professional career, which he was very humble about. His knowledge of repertoire, recordings and instruments was encyclopaedic. He treated everybody in the same way, a very generous and warm personality with a smile to accompany it. His sense of humour and ability to express the music that just poured out of him made him a unique communicator as a teacher and conductor. I don't think he realised how great his influence was in the Melbourne music-making scene.

The Blue Tin – Kirsty Bremner

Kirsty Bremner has been a member of the Melbourne Symphony Orchestra's first violin section since 1987. Guest appearances with other orchestras include the Australian Chamber Orchestra, the Malaysian Philharmonic Orchestra, Orchestra Ensemble Kanazawa in Japan, Sinfonia Britannia in Cardiff, Wales, and more recently the BBC Scottish Symphony Orchestra.

When Chris was auditioning for the National Music Camp, he came to Canberra where I grew up and accepted me for my first camp – it would have been in the late 1970s. I played in the orchestra that he conducted at camp and that's how I got to know him. He was extremely welcoming and warm and interested in us. Mentoring young people and having fun with them was very much his thing.

After leaving school, I studied music at the Tasmanian Conservatorium with Jan Sedivka and that's where I caught up with Chris again. He always came to Jan's Summer School, which was held immediately after the National Music Camp. People came to Hobart from all over Australia and New Zealand and there were quite a few from China as well. The string school centred around Jan Sedivka, and when he died, it was gone. It's sad, as that was the only one of international standing in Australia. It was superb.

Jan and Chris were very good friends. Chris often stayed with Jan in Hobart and Jan stayed with Chris in Melbourne. Chris had a collection of old *Strad* magazines* – really old ones. Jan used to drag a pile of them off to bed every night to read. I write articles for *In Tune*, the MSO Friends Society magazine, and one time was racking my brains looking for a topic. We had a visiting musician at the MSO who played a beautiful Stradivarius, so I decided to write about Stradavari and Guarneri instruments and who played them. Not knowing where to begin, I rang Chris and at the end of a forty-minute talk, I had my article. I didn't even have to open a book – other than to verify some of the details. He was spot on, of course; his knowledge was unbelievable.

In 2009, I was off work for some time with a badly fractured clavicle and managed to see Chris regularly. It was then that we became really close friends. We would meet for lunch, he would talk and I would listen. Chris would get annoyed with me sometimes because I didn't say much, but I was very happy to hear about his life, his stories and his views on the world. His interests and knowledge spread well beyond the world of music.

Not long before he died, he told me about Alma Rosé and the women's orchestra at Auschwitz. He wept as he talked about it. Growing up, he wouldn't have known many Jewish people but clearly he felt a great affinity with them – not only through marrying Annette but because almost every great violinist has been Jewish.

My last birthday was my fiftieth and Chris gave me a gift that he said was worth nothing in itself but worth everything to him. It was a little blue tin that had once contained gut strings made by an old craftsman who lived near Chris's home in England and whose business disappeared with the invention of modern strings. Ironically, since the revival of early music performances, people are buying gut strings again and this man's skill would be much sought after now. On the card that came with the tin, Chris wrote:

> To my dear Kirsty on the occasion of your 50th birthday. This little tin
> is certainly a hundred years old and I am sure the most useless gift you
> will receive. It has been with me some 65 years and I am very attached
> to it. I give it to you as some part of me and please look after it. At

the turn of the century, 1900, thousands of these little blue tins would have resided in the violin cases of violinists all over the world. They contained the most exquisite gut strings ever made. Just one set in each box. Old man Tom lived within eight miles of my home and had his workshop there. You will see the address: Wellington, Somerset, England. Whenever my friend Ron drove past Tom's house he would tell me about the old man, that with his own hand he had destroyed every piece of equipment used in the string making. Sadly, the coming of metal strings, nylon and synthetic etc meant that his market just faded out. I'm sure he died of a broken heart. So here is one of his little blue tins.

* *The Strad* is a magazine for string players, teachers, students, makers and dealers, and it has been in circulation since 1890.

Beyond Strings – Genevieve Lacey

Genevieve Lacey is a recorder virtuoso who has won multiple awards for her performances. She has been artistic director of the Melbourne Autumn Festival and the Four Winds Festival, sits on a number of arts boards and played with orchestras and chamber music ensembles around the world.

When I was a student at the Conservatorium, I really treasured Chris's passion for music and his ability to communicate that. It's hard to describe this, but he could get to the heart of any piece very easily. He was also an alarmingly perceptive listener. I suppose one of the ways that he and I connected is that we both have quite an emotional relationship with sound. I don't know how to describe that either, but it's a kindred spirit kind of thing, and you easily recognise it in someone else.

It always struck me that Chris, as a conductor, could very vividly hear sounds in his head. His imagination of how a piece could sound was powerful. That's exactly what you need when you're conducting or teaching, as well as the ability to communicate that. As a player, you develop that primarily through your instrument, but as a conductor of a not very good student orchestra, your imagination or 'inner ear' has to be pretty amazing.

The London String Quartet and later – Carl Pini

Carl Pini, violinist, led the London String Quartet before coming to Sydney in 1968, where he formed the Carl Pini Quartet and the Sinfonia of Sydney. Since then he has played with and conducted a number of orchestras, including the Philharmonia in London, the Hong Kong Philharmonic, the Melbourne Symphony Orchestra and the Sydney Symphony Orchestra. He is an honorary member of the Royal College of Music in London and has taught at universities in Australia and New Zealand.

My father, Anthony Pini, was principal cello in the Royal Philharmonic Orchestra formed by Sir Thomas Beecham in 1946. Before that, he was principal cello with the London Philharmonic, which Sir Thomas established in 1928. Dad was a distinguished soloist, appearing in various concerts at the BBC Proms fourteen times from 1942 to 1956, making many recordings of chamber music and the Elgar Cello Concerto. He was cellist in the Philharmonia Quartet when Henry Holst was leader. Henry taught Christopher Martin at the Royal College of Music.

When I was about twenty-five, I fell in love with a Carlo Bergonzi violin that I found at W.E. Hills of Bond Street. The price was £4,500 but I only had £2,500 and couldn't raise more. My father and I tried to borrow from the banks, but in those days bankers knew nothing about the value of musical instruments. Dad decided to ask Sir Thomas, who didn't hesitate. He wrote out a cheque for £2,000 and refused Dad's suggestion of a formal letter stating that he had lent us the money. In fact, we were able to pay the money back very quickly. Pinchas Zuckerman once advised me never to sell the Bergonzi. He was right. If I had it now, it would be worth a fortune.

I knew of Chris when he was playing in the Edinburgh String Quartet. At that stage, there were seventy or eighty music clubs in Britain and quartets had a viable income touring these. All the schools, too, had music clubs, and quartets like the Edinburgh String Quartet would have gone to music camps and festivals. There was also a lot of work with the BBC. I later heard that Chris was playing in the Netherlands Chamber Orchestra with Szymon Goldberg. Incidentally, Chris came to a concert at my school in Highgate, North London, to hear me play the Tchaikovsky concerto when I was sixteen.

Chris and I finally got to play together as musicians in the Philomusica of London, an offshoot of the Boyd Neel Orchestra which I had joined when I left the army. It was mostly strings and many of its players had been in the Air Force. Boyd was a doctor and not a very good conductor, but he learned how to mould this group which became famous. Our manager organised a tour of Switzerland, but forgot to factor in the fares so we were out of pocket. He got the sack and Boyd, a great friend of his, left and took his name with him. Most of the board resigned too.

Professor Thurston Dart from Cambridge University became our new artistic director and manager. He was an expert on baroque music and his books are still the standard works. He renamed the orchestra the Philomusica and got us to play using different bows in the shape of baroque bows specially made for us. It was a very stylish group. Cecil Aronowitz, another of Chris's teachers, was our principal viola.

When Professor Dart left, we had an interim period without an artistic director and Granville Jones, the first violin, took over temporarily. As the second seat in the first violins, I was his assistant. Granville was a wonderful player and musician but suffered from ill-health. I was left to do some of the organising. Cecil Aronowitz left during this time and I invited Chris to be principal viola. My colleagues wanted someone else, but I thought that Chris was the man – and he was. I was grateful to Chris for his contribution. His ideas were always worth following and I relied on him a lot.

Eventually George Malcolm, the harpsichordist, became our next artistic director but when the orchestra fell into financial difficulties, he left. I organised another director with access to money, a Danish-American amateur musician called Nils Gruen. We thought his money would help – which it did – but he insisted on conducting, which didn't help at all.

I became leader of the London String Quartet in 1960, reforming the group in 1966 and inviting Chris to play viola. It was a great success. Chris knew the repertoire so well. Unfortunately we didn't make any recordings, but we did give a memorable concert at the Queen Elizabeth Hall which included the famous viola solo which begins the Bartók Sixth Quartet. Of course, Chris played superbly.

One day out of the blue in 1968, I had an invitation to go to Sydney. I remember going to my next rehearsal with the quartet wondering how I was going to tell them. I just blurted it out, and Chris laughed and said that he himself was about to say exactly the same thing – he was going to Australia!

I came to Australia to join the Sydney String Quartet as first violin, which I think was a misjudgement on their part. They had a fine viola player, Robert Pikler, a Hungarian who had had a difficult war experience having been caught by the Japanese in Java and put in a camp. He had formed the Sydney String Quartet in the early 1960s.

When I arrived for our first rehearsal, we sat down to do to the Haydn C Major Quartet. I raised my bow and plunged in, but my surprise nobody else played. When I asked why, they told me that Robert was the one they followed. It was a good quartet but inevitably we had an unfortunate parting of the ways. I was asked to start my own group and I formed the Carl Pini String Quartet. At least two string quartets in Australia stopped playing in the early 1970s but we were very successful, with three overseas tours for Musica Viva and some recordings for HMV.

Chris and I didn't see an awful lot of each other in Australia. I was in Sydney, while he was in Melbourne. The first time I came to Melbourne was when Chris invited me to play with his University orchestra. We played the Bach D Minor Concerto, normally played on the harpsichord. Bach wrote a lot of concertos across the instruments; this was the greatest of them and the only time that I have ever played it. On another occasion, Chris invited me to do a concert with Annette playing Purcell Fantasias and trio sonatas. I had recorded a Purcell disc and knew his music well. During rehearsals, Annette had problems with some rhythms but when it came to the concert, I was the one who got lost. Annette was perfect. Chris never let me forget it!

My father-in-law, Don Hazelwood, is an icon in the music world in Sydney, just as my own father was to some extent in London. My wife, Jane Hazelwood, played at music camps and with the Australian Youth Orchestra (AYO). Chris Martin was a key figure and one of the first involved in auditioning young people for the National Music Camp and the AYO. The organisation was extremely well run and lots of professional musicians received their grounding there. Jane remembers Chris inspiring the students, who loved him and his stories, and she never forgot the Elgar *Enigma Variations* that he conducted.

Whenever I had an important solo or concerto to play, I asked Chris for advice. When I wanted to re-establish my own thoughts about music and what was happening in the music world, I would call him and we would talk for an hour or more. We also talked a lot about old times. Chris had a wonderful collection of records, CDs and videos, which I enjoyed when I stayed with him in Melbourne. Going to his place in Toorak was like coming home, and he will remain in my memory as a great friend, colleague and a refreshing and stimulating voice in the world of music.

The Zeitgeist – Hartmut Lindemann

Hartmut Lindemann is Professor of Viola at the Hochschule für Musik in the Westfälischen Wilhelms-Universität in Münster, Germany. He is regarded as one of the world's great viola players. He studied in Cologne and was principal viola with the North West German Philharmonic, the Tasmanian and Sydney Symphony Orchestras and the Australian Chamber Orchestra before embarking on a career as solo violist, chamber musician and teacher.

I met Chris in 1983 at the Jan Sedivka Summer School. He stood one evening in front of my door with a bottle of red wine and said, 'I hear that you like Thibaud'. From then on, we were in constant contact. I had recently arrived from Germany to take up the position of principal viola with the Tasmanian Symphony Orchestra. Sedivka, a Czech violinist, had established a distinguished string school in Hobart and his summer school was an important meeting place for interesting people.

Chris and I found that we shared exactly the same taste in music and a great love of the old violinists. There are five whom we both considered foundational: Mischa Elman, Jacques Thibaud, Josef Szigeti, Fritz Kreisler and Jascha Heifetz. Anything that has been done of any value since is based on these five characters. When Chris and I listened to music together and some beautiful detail would happen, like a portamento or a change in sound colour, we would catch each other's eyes and know that we both felt just as intently about it. Chris never had that with anybody else, nor did I, and I cannot imagine that I ever will again.

We loved the way these five players moved so beautifully on the violin. Shifting – which is how you connect one finger with the other – can be done in a clumsy way, a graceful way or with very clever fingering. It's like the difference between the walk of a graceful model and a farmer. No matter how agile the farmer, his movements will be clumsy in comparison.

The sound colouring, too, of these early violinists is amazing. They had such individuality that you would recognise after two notes who was playing. They actually did not have much in common in the physical way they played. The reason for this was that in the past there were national string schools and each had certain characteristics, so you had the Russian style of playing or the French or Belgian style, and so on. Jacques Thibaud, for example, was utterly French. His playing was like opening a bottle of perfume.

The big difference between Heifetz and the others is that Heifetz never gave up working on himself. With most other violinists, once they have recorded a piece it never gets better. With Heifetz, when he re-recorded a piece it was always better. He constantly worked on improving his playing. I think that Chris admired the unbelievable artistry that Heifetz had. Heifetz was the bridge – the last of the romantics and the first of the moderns. He had the precision of the new and the meaning of the old.

What I most admired about Chris was his musical instinct. He knew what was genuine and what was fake. There are so many musicians who look right on the outside and then they play a note and you know that it's a musical lie. Chris would never be fooled. I remember we were once driving somewhere listening to Vengerov's playing the *Symphonie Espagnole* by Lalo, and Chris thought it so hideous that he went to the trouble of calling the ABC and telling them never to put it on again. It was not the playing that he objected to – Vengerov is a brilliant violinist – it was the taste and style. Chris felt that it was artificial and misrepresented the music.

Chris and I loved playing that reflected the spirit of the times, the *Zeitgeist*. Kreisler's recordings, for example, speak of life in Vienna at the end of the Danube monarchies. Those five great players were in fact closer to the time when the great classical pieces were written. It is harder to get the *Zeitgeist* right now, in 2012.

Chris used to say, 'I don't know what a good musician is. What is a good musician?' Is it a dramatic and charismatic player like Ivry Gitlis, for example? You could disagree with a lot of things he does on stage, but the audience eats out of his hand. Is that a good musician? Then you can have a musician like Heifetz, with divine phrasing played in a visually restrained way. For Chris, music was essentially sensuous, not an intellectual thing. It was to do with the sound and warmth of the playing. I have seen him moved to tears by music. I loved that about him.

Chris and I had a surprising amount in common. We both came from little towns; we both came from lower income families; we both, strangely enough, played on the local rubbish tip shooting rats with air-rifles. For both of us, our lives changed when we discovered music and we were given the opportunity to develop our playing – Chris through his sponsorship from the lace factory and me through a government music scholarship readily available in Germany for underprivileged children.

Whenever he played for fun, Chris always took out the violin, never the viola. Chris played the viola but he adored the violin. The violin was his first instrument, whereas I started on the viola so I didn't have the luxury of choosing between the two. I always tried to play in a way Chris liked, using elements that he admired in those great players. I was once accused by a critic of 'beautifully old-fashioned playing'. I didn't care. I played the way that I felt I should. Chris would watch me and occasionally make some comment, suggesting that I try this or that. He told me that no one played the viola as I did. I think that I realised in my playing some of his ideas.

Chris conducted often for me; the last concert was the Bartók concerto with the Corpus Medicorum. He was a good conductor, very good, although towards the end he suffered from impaired hearing, which he found frustrating.

When Chris had his terrible battle with cancer in 2001, I took some time off work during the vacation breaks to come to Melbourne and stay with him. He was terribly affected by the chemotherapy but never realised how sick he was. At one stage, all the doctors said that he had only two more weeks to live. He agreed to be a guinea-pig for an experimental drug that hadn't been officially released at that time, and the miracle happened. He gained ten more years of life.

One of the most amazing things about Chris was how he managed to play the Mozart Concertante when he was eighty with Spiros Rantos, even though he hadn't touched the viola for years. He took it up again, got into shape and played for the anniversary concert with the Chamber Strings of Melbourne. He had incredible will power, but all the will power in the world would not have made any difference if he hadn't had a natural talent.

Chris's greatest impact in Australia was on the amateur music scene. He was able to get a decent sound out of any group and was able to lead players into the middle of the music. He was an incredibly talented man with great presence but was not about proving himself. He wanted to be loved by people and largely succeeded in that.

He was also a born performer. On his very last public appearance in August 2011, Chris spun an obviously invented story about his native Devon and how the village idiots used to sing the 'Idiot Song'. He sang it in the local dialect. You can see it on YouTube. It was very funny, but there was something about the way he waved goodbye to the audience afterwards that told you that he wouldn't be seen on the podium again. For someone who was so depleted of energy, to get up there and give a performance like that was incredible.

Chris and I spoke almost every day. After breakfast, I would make myself a cup of tea and go to the phone and call him. For weeks after he died, I often burst into tears in the mornings. That's when I decided to learn the Walton concerto. Instead of missing Chris, I would sit down and fill the void with music that he loved. I was able to play it with Chris's son Ben at a small concert in Chris's honour when I next visited Australia in March 2012. I noticed that Chris was completely missed by the other musicians there. Nobody will take his place.

The Chamber Strings of Melbourne – Dr Alexandra Cameron MBE

Dr Cameron was born in Queensland in 1910 and has spent a lifetime in music education, including twenty years with the Education Department of Victoria as Inspector of Music. She started the Saturday Music School in 1967, for children from all schools to play together in an orchestra or band, and out of this grew the Melbourne Youth Orchestra. She founded the Chamber Strings of Melbourne in 1980.

I met Chris in 1983 when he took over the conducting of the Chamber Strings of Melbourne. We rehearsed at University High School every Sunday before moving to Methodist Ladies' College. Chris conducted the orchestra for nearly thirty years, with a short break when he asked Spiros Rantos to take over because he felt that a change would be good for the orchestra. When Spiros went to Brisbane, Chris came back.

The reason we chose Chris was because our conductor, Harry Hutchins, recommended him. Chris was a real gentleman: kindly, thoughtful, nothing too much trouble. As a conductor, he was always on time and never left early. If there was a concert coming up, he'd look up a number of works, come and see me and discuss the programme. If he wanted something that we didn't have in our library, we'd hire or buy a copy for every child. There are usually about twenty-four players in the orchestra, mostly aged between fifteen and twenty-one, although some are a bit older. We always paid our conductor, but everyone else involved in supporting the orchestra is honorary.

When I began the orchestra, I had just finished working in the Education Department and was on the Board of Inspectors. I arrived home from my last meeting when there was a knock on my door. It was a group of boys from the Melbourne Youth Orchestra, who said, 'Now that you've got nothing to do, will you start a string orchestra so that we can learn the repertoire?' I have written out the story of the Chamber Strings of Melbourne and my niece is in the process of typing the manuscript. It will be called *The Chamber Strings of Melbourne: Thirty Years of Music Making – 1980–2010. A Story Culled from Happy Memories.* I am hoping that it will be ready at the end of the year.

The Chamber Strings did a lot of overseas tours, which Chris and I would plan together. He was involved in everything to do with the orchestra. When we decided where we wanted to go, we would get in touch with local people and work from there. In Vienna, we entered an international competition and were not surprised to win our section. We knew that we were good. We played Sculthorpe's *Port Essington* as our Australian choice. What came as a shock was winning the Mayor of Vienna's Special Prize for the whole competition.

We were always guided by the three aims set out in our constitution: first, to form a string orchestra for gifted and intelligent students who wished to study the string repertoire; second, to achieve excellence in performances; and third, to travel overseas as the opportunity afforded to widen the participants' horizons. They would pay about two-thirds of the cost. I sponsored the rest. It was a great experience for them, some say one of the highlights of their lives. Among the countries we toured were

Poland, Italy, Greece, Russia, England and Scotland. We always explored the local history and culture.

Christopher had a big place in the music world in Australia. He was among the best musicians and highly respected. He conducted the Melbourne Doctors' Orchestra and the Australian Doctors' Orchestra, which made him honorary conductor for life.

He was somewhat conservative in his choice of composers but always included at least one English composer, such as Elgar, Benjamin Britten or Vaughan Williams. He had a high regard for the Australian composer Malcolm Williamson, who lived in England, and also liked Peter Sculthorpe.

It's important for a conductor to know the players, especially with a young orchestra. Chris knew them all by name. He was very impatient with anyone who was disruptive and he kept strict discipline. If one of the players needed extra help, he would see them at home for nothing. Largely as a result of Chris's work, the Chamber Strings of Melbourne is considered the best amateur chamber music group in the city.

National Music Camp – Jenny Johnson

Jenny Johnson was born in Melbourne in 1935 and studied the violin with her mother, Bessie Heath, a member of the Melbourne Symphony Orchestra. She had a career in early childhood education but her heart was in music and she was involved in the running of the State and National Music Camps for fifteen years. She is a founding member of the Stonnington Symphony Orchestra and the Chamber Music Summer School at Mount Buller.

In his gentle way, Christopher Martin affected a lot of people. I came to know him well through my involvement in the administration of the State and National Music Camps. He never had a sense of his own importance. You could sit and talk to him whether you were on the staff or one of the students – he treated everybody the same. He usually took the third orchestra – the least experienced of the players but still of a high standard. One thing I noticed over the years was that the standard of the National Music Camp rose higher and they started to bring in conductors from overseas. Of the three performances at the final concert, Chris's orchestra for me was always the most moving.

Somehow he had the ability to get the most musical performances from his players.

It would be hard to underestimate the influence of those music camps on the development of music in Australia. Certainly, of my generation there would be few professional and skilled amateur musicians who did not attend at least one. I was lucky enough to go to five music camps; that couldn't happen today when the competition to get in is so fierce.

My mother saw an article in the newspaper about music camps and wrote and enquired. The first two had been held in the late 1940s at Point Lonsdale, under the auspices of the National Fitness Association and the Victorian School Music Association. A third was planned for 1952 at Geelong Grammar School and I went. There were more than a hundred students, mostly from Victoria. A number of them later joined the Melbourne Symphony Orchestra.

Hephzibah Menuhin was living in the Western District at that time, and she came and played a beautiful Mozart concerto with us. She also gave us a talk one afternoon about her life on the property. She didn't believe in having paid staff, she told us, so she did everything herself. She didn't use sugar in any of her cooking, because she said that it wasn't good for you. She was very involved in starting up things to help isolated women in the country, like travelling libraries and get-togethers. She was well ahead of her time in that way.

The structure of our day at the music camp was a tutorial in the morning – in which groups such as first violins, violas or cellos worked with a professional musician – and then two orchestral sessions. It was quite common to have a tutor demonstrating with a cigarette in his mouth. We would watch fascinated as the ash got longer and longer and eventually fell into the 'F' hole of his instrument.

Afternoons were free, but there were organised activities such as swimming or walking or playing, practising or playing chamber music with friends. At 5 o'clock we had student chamber music, known as 'cocktail concerts', and after dinner the staff performed more chamber music.

Over the years, the daily pattern has remained basically the same. What has changed dramatically is the number of students attending and the standard of their ability and the overall quality of teaching. There are now about 230 students at National Music Camp. When Chris was involved, numbers would have been around 150. Chris was always outstanding as a tutor and conductor, but he also did a huge job assessing applicants. Getting into the National Music Camp became highly competitive and Chris would travel from state to state to audition students. He had an innate ability to see the musicality of a player – which some people can pick even in young children. The auditions were held under great scrutiny and there was always somebody from the local state sitting in.

At the end of my involvement with music camps and at a time when my children no longer needed me so much, a group of friends and I decided to form a new orchestra. Some of us had played with the Australian Youth Orchestra and knew what it was like to work hard and put on a performance. We were frustrated with the quality of local orchestras around – such as the South Melbourne and the Kew – as members didn't practise and were increasingly social. We wanted six rehearsals, a performance and then a break. Rather than have a resident conductor, we decided that inviting different conductors would give us more scope. This was the beginning of the Malvern Orchestra, now known as Stonnington Symphony Orchestra.

Chris often conducted for us and we always loved working with him. He chose wonderful programmes, always including some English music. We once did a work with him by Vaughan Williams, called *Job*. Chris brought in his bible sometimes and read the relevant passages, such as the one about Job's being tormented by boils. He explained that this was what the music was describing. It was eye-opening, this music. I have never heard it performed before or since.

At about the time we started the Malvern Orchestra in the early 1980s, I was involved in another exciting new musical adventure. This was the Chamber Music Summer School at Mount Buller. This came about after a quartet I played in went to the New England School of Music Summer School. We got to know Janis Laurs, the cellist who played with the quartet in residence. It was an extremely fine quartet and did a lot of touring with Musica Viva.

When Janis got the appointment as associate principal cellist with the Melbourne Symphony Orchestra, the quartet split up and he and his partner initially stayed with Roy Bull, near my own home in Malvern. We all made music together and talked over ideas for playing more chamber music. Janis was a great motivator and he and Roy rushed off around Victoria looking for suitable places for a summer school. A friend suggested one of the ski lodges at Mount Buller and it turned out to be perfect. I was involved in the running of the Chamber Music Summer School for twenty-five years.

The Mount Buller Summer School was always relatively small, with a delightfully intimate setting. We started with ten groups and never had more than a dozen. People came from all over, because of the calibre of tutors we had. We also had a scholarship gift fund, with which we sponsored two student quartets each year. The Flinders String Quartet came one year, and another we had the Tinalley String Quartet. They were both brilliant. Chris came for years. If he wasn't tutoring, he would come as a visitor. He loved to sit and talk to people.

I didn't study music at the Conservatorium but I did go there for lessons at lunchtime, first of all with Basil Jones, who became director of the Queensland Conservatorium, and then with Boris Stupel – both of whom I met at National Music Camps. Boris Stupel survived Dachau and came to Australia after the war. He told me that in the camp, the guards smashed his instruments in front of him. I studied violin with him and he told me that in Europe, most violinists also played the viola. He gave me a viola and I learned that, too.

Some years later I went to Chris for more viola lessons, and he showed me a beautiful violin and viola that he had acquired from a deceased estate. They were made by Charles Adolphe Maucotel. The viola was unusually small and Chris agreed to sell it to me. I still play it. It brings back many memories.

University of the Third Age Orchestra – Ruth Muir

Ruth Muir is the manager of the Orchestra of University of the Third Age, Hawthorn.

Not long after I joined the University of the Third Age (U3A), Hawthorn, in 1996 the president, Jean Giese, asked for my help in forming a U3A Chamber Orchestra. It had long been a dream of hers and, as I was a pianist and a music-lover, she thought that I might know of a possible conductor. As it happened, I did know George Logie-Smith who had been director of Music at Scotch College when my boys were there. He had also conducted the Astra Chamber Orchestra for many years. At that stage, he was retired and somewhat reluctant to pick up his baton once more, but his wife encouraged him to do it and we gathered together a group of about sixteen musicians. Several of them had played with George before, including his friend, the cellist Annette Martin.

Rehearsals started in mid-1997 at the Oxley Road Uniting Church. I had no previous experience in running an orchestra, having been just a member of the audience, but I learned 'on the hoof'. We gave our first concert in October 1997 at the Hawthorn Town Hall and, with a few exceptions, have performed there regularly ever since. After about eighteen months George, who was in his eighties, had to leave the orchestra because of his failing health and Annette suggested her husband, Christopher Martin, as a possible replacement. Chris had just retired from the Conservatorium and was overseas at the time, but talked to me on his return and agreed to take us on. He began rehearsing with us in March 2000, and apart from one year off when he was ill, he stayed for ten years, conducting twenty-three concerts for us.

It was miraculous how people started flocking to the orchestra. They came from all over the place and in no time we had more than fifty players, ranging from people in their late fifties and early sixties to several in their eighties and even one in her nineties. They were a mixture of retired professionals, gifted amateurs and even a few who had not been learning long. Although I had not met Chris myself before he came to us, he was well known in music circles and many of our members knew him or knew of him.

What people found so attractive about Chris was that he was a 'people person', had a light touch and a great sense of humour, but above all there was his profound musicianship. The more you knew him, the more you realised how deep this was. He was always encouraging and would often grab the violin from the leader to demonstrate the bowing. He respected all our players regardless of ability and they, in turn, adored him.

When a group of brass players joined the orchestra, Chris found it hard to choose programmes which the strings could play comfortably and which included the brass. We couldn't do the big symphonies, and though we performed a lot of Haydn, Schubert, Mozart and the early Beethovens, they rarely included brass. Chris worried about it a lot and found it quite a burden. I would try to reassure him by saying, 'They can't all play everything in the whole programme, they'll understand'. He was so anxious not to hurt people's feelings, not to put them down, always to include them – he was very thoughtful and really cared about the orchestra.

Chris could always find soloists, as he knew so many fine young musicians. He would call on players from the Chamber Strings of Melbourne or draw on one of his other contacts, such as past students from the Conservatorium. It worked very well and I thought it was particularly appropriate to have young musicians performing with an older orchestra. What also worked well was Chris's story-telling. We soon learned that we had to set up a microphone for him at concerts, as he would roam up and down the aisle and lots of people couldn't hear him. He would never do a concert without talking to the audience. The stories poured out of him, but he never really adjusted to the microphone!

Soon after he started with us, Chris became ill with cancer and was away for a year. He was very sick and the chemotherapy nearly destroyed him. We were struggling with guest conductors and wondered if Chris would ever come back. I felt strongly that I had to keep the orchestra going, and amazingly Chris did recover and came back. The orchestra gained a fine reputation under his direction and built up a strong local following. Our programme notes for the first concert after his death encapsulate this:

> In his ten years with us as director of music, Chris helped the orchestra to grow and develop into the unique instrument it has become: a united body of musicians from very differing backgrounds and levels of ability, all working and playing for the sheer love of shared music-making – a quality which personified 'our Chris'. We will always miss him and dedicate today's concert to his memory.

Some years ago, one of our cellists, Margot Bremner, suggested that we do something about getting Chris an honour in acknowledgement of his work with community orchestras such as ours. We went ahead and got all the papers, reading through them carefully to discover that the recipient had to be an Australian citizen – so that was the end of that. Chris was adamant about retaining his British citizenship. He played very little Australian music other than Percy Grainger, whose arrangement for the 'Londonderry Air' he loved. The music he chose for his final concert is typical of his taste; it included Walton, Vivaldi, Schubert, Bach, Elgar and Johann Strauss.

In his later years, Chris would sometimes arrive at the hall for the morning rehearsal looking dreadful – pale and weak. He would say that he wasn't feeling very well, then he would pick up his baton, talk to the players, and begin. It was like watering a drooping plant. His face would fill out, his voice would get stronger, his eyes would dance. He was alive again. It was the music; it just fed him.

Coda

An imaginary conversation between Chris and Ben:

'It's called *In the Middle of the Music*.'
'Am I in it?'

'It's about you, Dad.'
'About me is it? Who wrote it?'

'It's a compilation.'
'A com-pi-la-tion. So a lot about me, then.'

'There are a fair number of contributions.'
'Well that's good, isn't it? Should I be thanking anyone?'

'I think they're thanking you, Dad.'

Notes

1   Imogen Holst (1907–84), British conductor and composer, was closely associated with her father's work. She went to Aldeburgh in 1952 to work with Benjamin Britten and was artistic director of the festival from 1956 to 1977. She lived there for the rest of her life. In 1953, she formed the Purcell Singers and conducted them until 1967. She is buried in the churchyard at St Peter and St Paul's Anglican Church at Aldeburgh, behind the graves of Benjamin Britten and Peter Pears.

2   A booklet, 'Gustav Holst and Thaxted' by Imogen Holst, giving an account of Holst's association with the village is available in the Thaxted Parish Church.

3   The Amadeus was one of the great quartets of the twentieth century. Three of its players – Norbert Brainin, Siegmund Nissel and Peter Schidlof – were Jewish refugees interred in Britain during World War II. Together with cellist Martin Lovett they formed the Brainin Quartet in 1947, which they renamed the Amadeus Quartet the following year. The Amadeus became the leading quartet in Europe, made numerous recordings and received many honours including the OBE in Britain and the Great Cross of Merit in Germany. It disbanded in 1987 on the death of the viola player, Peter Schidlof.

4   See Ron Davey, *Batons and Bows: The Story of the Tiverton Youth Orchestra*, Kelly Publications, Tiverton, 2002.

5   Angel Grande (1895–1951) was born in Madrid and is known for introducing new Spanish works into England and English works into Spain. He had an outstanding career as a violinist and later as a conductor and composer.

6   Apart from childhood lessons from his father, Albert Sammons (1886–1957) was virtually self-taught. He left school at the age of twelve to become a professional musician and played in bands, orchestras and musical soirées. In 1909, he was invited by Thomas Beecham to join the Beecham Symphony Orchestra. In 1910, he formed the London String Quartet and in 1921, the Chamber Music Players. He was closely associated with English music and worked with Frederick Delius on the composition of a violin concerto. He also composed a number of pieces for violin and piano and, from 1939, he taught at the Royal College of Music. On his death, Sir Adrian Boult called him 'a great musician in every sense of the word'.

7   Henry Holst was born in Copenhagen in 1899, led the Berlin Philharmonic from 1922 to 1931 and was a founding member in Britain, with other members of the Liverpool Philharmonic Orchestra, of the Philharmonia Quartet.

8   Sir Neville Marriner, born in 1924, was an English violinist and conductor. He both studied and taught at the Royal College of Music in London and attended Pierre Monteux's Summer School in Maine, where he took lessons in conducting. In 1959, he formed the Academy of St Martin-in-the-Fields. Between 1969 and 1978, he was the first music director of the Los Angeles Chamber Orchestra; from 1979 to 1986, the music director of the Minnesota Orchestra; from 1986 to 1989, the principal conductor of the Stuttgart Radio Symphony Orchestra. He recorded for a number of labels and was one of the most influential conductors of his day.

9   Composed by Grigoraş Dinicu for his graduation from the Bucharest Conservatory in 1906, it was rearranged by Jascha Heifetz in 1932.
10   Chris Martin arranged for this piece to be played at his funeral.
11   A distinguished viola player, Cecil Aronowitz (1916–78) was co-founder of the Melos Ensemble, a leading chamber musician and influential teacher at the Royal College of Music from 1948 to 1973. A number of composers wrote for him, including Benjamin Britten.
12   Born in in Hungary in 1881, Béla Bartók is considered one of the greatest composers of the twentieth century. He first studied piano but was soon writing small compositions. Early influences were a growing love of folk music and Debussy, to whose work his friend Kodály introduced him. In 1907, he taught at the Royal Academy in Budapest. Fritz Reiner, George Solti and Lili Kraus were among his students. He also became a prolific composer during the first decades of the twentieth century, writing a wide range of works including an opera, *Bluebeard's Castle,* and a ballet, *The Miraculous Mandarin.* Although not Jewish, he hated the Nazis and left Hungary for the USA in 1940 – the year during which his health began to deteriorate. In his last two years, he wrote some of his greatest pieces including *Concerto for Orchestra, Sonata for Solo Violin* commissioned by Yehudi Menuhin and *Piano Concerto No. 3.* He died in 1945, leaving his viola concerto unfinished.
13   Joan Dickson, born in Edinburgh in 1921, was a professor at the Royal College of Music in London and an outstanding cello teacher and a fine performer. She died in London in 1994.
14   [no copy in MS note; to come? or delete?]
15   Hester Dickson was born in Edinburgh in 1924. Her musical career paralleled that of her sister Joan and they regularly performed duets together. Since 1969, Hester was on the staff of the Royal Scottish Academy of Music and Drama and she was awarded an honorary degree in 2009, at the age of eighty-five.
16   Sir Adrian Boult (1889–1983) was one of the great English conductors. He is particularly noted for training the newly formed BBC Symphony Orchestra in 1930, which quickly gained an international reputation under his baton.
17   Adila (1886–1962) was the older sister of Jelly. She studied at the Budapest Academy under Hubay and with Joseph Joachim in Berlin. Joachim left her his 1715 Stradivari violin. She settled in England in 1913 and married Alexandre Fachiri in 1919. The sisters were noted for their duo performances and gave their last public performance in 1960. They played the Bach Double Violin Concerto.
18   Ernő Dohnányi (1877–1960) was born into an aristocratic Hungarian family and made his debut as a pianist in Berlin in 1897. Following this, he had a brilliant international career. He became director of the Budapest Philharmonic Orchestra in 1919, promoting Hungarian composers and musicians. He disbanded the orchestra in 1941 in protest against anti-Jewish legislation. He did what he could to protect Jewish musicians. After the war, he settled in America.
19   The Griller Quartet was formed in 1931 in England, with Sidney Griller as first violin, Jack O'Brian on second violin, Philip Burton on viola and Colin Hampton on cello. The quartet played together for thirty years, made numerous recordings and was quartet-in-residence at the University of California from 1949 to 1961.
20   The eminent violinist and conductor Szymon Goldberg (1909–93) was born in Poland and studied in Germany, where he was concert master of the Dresden State Orchestra (1925–29) and the Berlin Philharmonic (1929–34). During the war, he toured the Far East with Lili Kraus and was interned by the Japanese. Afterwards he visited Australia

before settling in America. He founded the Netherlands Kamer Orkest (Chamber Orchestra) in Amsterdam in 1955 and led it for twenty-two years. He married Japanese pianist Miyoko Yamane, and died in Japan at the age of eighty-four.

21 Born in 1921 in London, Dennis Brain came from an exceptionally musical family and was the third generation to play the horn. He had a brilliant career and played with some of the leading conductors of his day, including Herbert von Karajan and Karl Haas. Benjamin Britten wrote 'Serenade for Tenor, Horn and Strings' for him and Peter Pears. He was a musical celebrity and became something of a legend after his tragic death in 1957, at the age of thirty-six.

22 The Melbourne Symphony Orchestra was founded by Alberto Zelman in 1906 and is the oldest professional orchestra in Australia. It became one of the ABC Radio orchestras in 1934, changed its name to Victorian Symphony Orchestra in 1949 and changed it back in 1965. Conductors have included Sir Bernard Heinze (1937–50), Walter Susskind (1954–55), Willem van Otterloo (1967–70), Hiroyuki Iwaki (1974–97) and Markus Stenz (1998–2004).

23 After studying violin in Paris in the 1920s, Georges Tzipine (1907–78) moved to conducting as well as composing background music for documentary films. He conducted the principal French orchestras, the Hallé, BBC Philharmonic and Royal Liverpool Philharmonic in England. He was chief conductor for the Victorian (later Melbourne) Symphony Orchestra from 1960 to 1965.

24 Paul McDermott studied violin at the Melbourne Conservatorium in the 1940s and, among other musicians, was head-hunted by Sir Malcolm Sargent after World War II. He was offered the position of leader of the Scottish National Orchestra. Within six months, Sir Thomas Beecham invited him to be principal violin for the Royal Philharmonic. He returned to Melbourne in 1950, formed the Paul McDermott String Quartet and joined the Victorian (later Melbourne) Symphony Orchestra. He formed the Australian Musicians Guild in 1969 and started Music in the Round in 1972. It ceased two years after his death in 1983.

25 Born in London in 1947, David Helfgott was a child prodigy and won several local piano competitions including the State finals of the ABC's Instrumental and Vocal Competition six times. He went to the Royal College of Music in London at the age of nineteen and studied under Cyril Smith, winning a number of awards including the Dannreuther Prize for Best Concerto Performance. He played Rachmaninov's Piano Concerto No. 3. At the same time, he began experiencing the symptoms of mental illness that cut short his career. He slowly resumed his musical life in the 1980s and in 1996 his life was the subject of the film *Shine*, following which he embarked on a series of international performances. He continues to perform both in Australia and overseas.

26 *The Naked Island* by Russell Braddon was published by Werner Laurie, in London, in 1952.

27 Jacqueline du Pré (1945–87) began learning the cello at the age of four and made her debut at the Wigmore Hall at the age of sixteen. This was the start of an extraordinary career. Rostropovich regarded her as the only cellist of her generation who could overtake his own achievement. She married pianist Daniel Barenboim in Jerusalem in 1967. She first experienced symptoms of multiple sclerosis in 1971 and was diagnosed with the disease in 1973. She died tragically young, fourteen years later, at the age of forty-two.

28 Die Wiener Walzermädeln.

29 See her book *Inherit the Truth: A Memoir of Survival and the Holocaust,* by Anita Lasker-Wallfisch, Thomas Dunne Books, 2000.

30   Hilary and Piers du Pré, *A Genius in the Family: An Intimate Memoir of Jacqueline du Pré*, Chatto & Windus, 1997.
31   John Kennedy (1922–80) was born in London and studied at the Royal Academy of Music, becoming the first cello with the Liverpool Philharmonic Orchestra in 1946 and the youngest principal in the United Kingdom at the time. His parents were both Australian: his mother Dorothy was a pianist who taught Caruso's children; his father Lauri was principal cellist with the BBC Symphony Orchestra under Sir Adrian Boult. They returned to Australia in 1944 and John joined them in 1958 and taught at the University of Melbourne Conservatorium until he retired in 1979, due to ill health. His children include the bassist Debbie Kennedy, cellist Lauren Kennedy, Erica Kennedy, violinist with the Flinders String Quartet, and solo performing violinist Nigel Kennedy.
32   Emmanuel Hurwitz (1919–2006) was born in London and became one of England's great chamber musicians. At fourteen years of age he won a scholarship to the Royal Academy of London and at eighteen was offered work with the London Philharmonic Orchestra under Sir Thomas Beecham. He spent the war years playing quartets and concerts for the troops. For the remainder of his life, he played with outstanding chamber music groups – including the Melos Ensemble and the Aeolian String Quartet – as well as leading the English Chamber Orchestra for many years and the New Philharmonia Orchestra under Otto Klemperer for two years. He taught at the Royal Academy of Music, was string coach for the Ernest Read Musical Association, made numerous recordings and was also famous for his masterclasses in Monterosso, in Italy.
33   Born in Liverpool in 1912, Frederick Riddle studied at the Royal College of Music from 1928 to 1933, then had a solo career with the London Symphony Orchestra before becoming principal viola with the London Philharmonic Orchestra in 1938. In 1953, he joined the Royal Philharmonic Orchestra under Sir Thomas Beecham. He died in 1995.
34   Harry Blech was born in London in 1910, showed early promise in the violin which he took up professionally but switched to conducting in his thirties. In 1949, he was asked by pianist Dorothea Braus to form an orchestra with which she could play two Mozart concertos. The first concert, which included two Mozart symphonies, was such a success that Blech realised he had found an audience for the Viennese composers he loved. The London Mozart Players continues to this day. Blech was much loved in the orchestral world in England for his good humour, his popular concerts and his encouragement of young musicians. He died in London in 1999.
35   Born in Vienna in 1912, Henry Krips emigrated to Australia in 1938. From 1948 to 1972 he was principal conductor of the West Australian Symphony Orchestra, and over the same period was also principal conductor of the South Australian Symphony Orchestra. From 1972, he conducted mainly in Europe. He composed a number of pieces including opera, ballets, songs and instrumental pieces. His composition *This Land of Mine* won one of many national anthem competitions but was never taken up. He was awarded honorary membership of the international Gustav Mahler Society, Vienna, in 1963 for his work in introducing Australian audiences to the composer. He died in Adelaide in 1987.
36   Eugene Goossens (1893–1962) was born in London and won a scholarship to the Royal College of Music at the age of fourteen. He studied composing and violin. He played with Thomas Beecham's Queen's Hall Orchestra before deciding to concentrate on conducting. He conducted orchestras round the world and was invited to become conductor for the Sydney Symphony Orchestra in 1947. In 1956, he came to the attention of the police because of his friendship with Rosaleen Norton, the 'Witch of Kings Cross'. His bags were searched at Sydney Airport on his return from a trip to

London and pornographic material was found. Goossens was charged, pleaded guilty and fined £100. He left Australia in disgrace. As well as a fine conductor, he was a noted composer and while in Sydney played a key role in pushing for a music performance venue, insisting that it be built at Bennelong Point.

37   See Elinor Morrisby, *Up Is Down: A Life of Violinist Jan Sedivka*, Lyrebird Press, Melbourne, 2006.

38   Born in the Rhineland, Markus Stenz studied music in Cologne and at Tanglewood with Leonard Bernstein. He was artistic director of the Montepulciano Festival from 1989 to 1995 and principal conductor of the London Sinfonietta from 1994 to 1998. He was artistic director and chief conductor of the Melbourne Symphony Orchestra from 1998 to 2004, during which time he took the MSO on its first European tour and appointed Brett Dean as composer-in-residence. He has since been principal conductor of the Gürzenich Orchestra (2005–09), principal guest conductor with the Hallé Orchestra (2009) and chief conductor with Radio Filharmonisch Orkest (2012–15).

39   Nicolette Fraillon studied violin, piano and viola and conducted her first concert at the age of sixteen. She graduated from Melbourne University Conservatorium in 1982 and went on to study in Vienna as well as perform with a number of European chamber orchestras, settling in the Netherlands in 1990. She was music director and principal conductor of the Netherlands National Ballet from 1993 to 1998, and director of the School of Music at the Australian National University from 1998 to 2002. In 2003, she took up the position of music director and chief conductor of the Australian Ballet.

40   For Ron Davey's account of this event, see *Batons and Bows*, pp. 49–59.

41   See *Concert Pitch: The Story of the National Music Camp Association and the Australian Youth Orchestra*, June Epstein, Hyland House, Melbourne, 1984.

42   Born in Germany in 1955, Wolfram Christ enjoyed a highly successful career as a viola player. Principal violist with the Berlin Philharmonic from 1978 to 1999, he was artistic director and advisor to the Sydney Music Conservatory from 1995 to 2000 and has held a professorship in viola at the Freiburg Musikhochschule since 1999. He has made numerous, widely acclaimed recordings.

43   *From Mao to Mozart* is a film of Isaac Stern's tour of China in 1980, in which he both performs with and teaches young Chinese musicians.

44   A repetiteur is a pianist who accompanies and coaches singers in an opera company. They develop a broad range of skills – playing, sight-reading and conducting – as well as interpreting works and communicating with performers.

45   István Kertész was born in Budapest in 1929. Most of his family died in Auschwitz but he was able to continue his musical studies. After the war, he studied violin, piano, composition and conducting at the Hungarian Royal Academy of Music and was strongly influenced by Bruno Walter and Otto Klemperer. Particularly known for his brilliant conducting of opera (his wife, Edith Gabry, was an operatic soprano), he worked with the Budapest Opera Orchestra, the Hamburg State Opera and Cologne Opera as well as other international companies. He was appointed director of the Cologne Opera in 1964, and he retained this position when he became principal conductor of the London Symphony Orchestra from 1965 to 1968. He was a frequent guest conductor to major orchestras worldwide and is noted for his many recordings, especially his interpretation of Bartók. He died in 1973.

46   Born in the Ukraine in 1928, Nelli Shkolnikova entered the Moscow Conservatory at the age of five to study violin and played her first concerto at eight. Her international career was launched in 1953 at the age of twenty-five, when she won the Marguerite Long–Jacques Thibaud Competition in Paris. She played with major orchestras around

the world until 1970, when she was forbidden to leave the Soviet Union. In 1982, she was finally allowed to play in West Berlin and defected. She accepted an invitation from conductor John Hopkins to teach at the Victorian College of the Arts and settled in Melbourne until 1987 when, at the recommendation of Isaac Stern, she was invited to become a professor of violin at the Jacobs School of Music at Indiana University. She retired to Melbourne in 2005 and died of cancer in 2010.

47   *The Story of Two Thousand Concerts* by Frank V. Hawkins, South Place Ethical Society, London, 1969.

48   The Wigmore Hall was built by the Bechstein firm in 1901, designed by English architect Thomas Colcutt. Originally called Bechstein Hall, it was Renaissance in style and intended to combine both grandeur and intimacy. It was sold in 1916 because of the anti-German feeling in England during the war and then was renamed after Wigmore Street. The Hall has featured most of the great musicians of the day, as well as rising artists. Performers particularly love the rapport between audiences and musicians. In 2005 the Hall's own label, Wigmore Hall Live, was launched to take its music beyond the confines of the building.

Index